Making Crafts from Your Kids' Art

Making Crafts from Your Kids' Art

Valerie Van Arsdale Shrader

LARK BOOKS

A Division of Sterling Publishing Co., Inc.
New York

Art Director: Dana Irwin
Photographer: keithwright.com
Cover Designer: Barbara Zaretsky
Assistant Art Director: Hannes Charen
Assistant Editor: Rain Newcomb
Illustrator: Orrin Lundgren
Production Assistance: Lorelei Buckley,
Shannon Yokeley
Editorial Assistance: Delores Gosnell,
Rosemary Kast

Special Photography:

Sanoma Syndication
Bart Brussee, 15, 23; Reneé Frinkling, 18

Library of Congress has cataloged the hardcover edition as follows:

Shrader, Valerie Van Arsdale.
    Making crafts from your kids' art / by Valerie Van Arsdale Shrader.-
    p. cm.
    ISBN 1-57990-368-1
    1. Handicraft. 2. Children's art. I. Title.

TT157.S5235 2003
745.5--dc21   2002043643

10 9 8 7 6 5 4 3 2 1

Published by Lark Books, a division of
Sterling Publishing Co., Inc.
387 Park Avenue South, New York, N.Y. 10016

First Paperback Edition 2005
© 2003, Lark Books

Distributed in Canada by Sterling Publishing,
c/o Canadian Manda Group, 165 Dufferin Street
Toronto, Ontario, Canada M6K 3H6

Distributed in the U.K. by Guild of Master Craftsman Publications Ltd.,
Castle Place, 166 High Street, Lewes, East Sussex, England BN7 1XU
Tel: (+ 44) 1273 477374, Fax: (+ 44) 1273 478606,
Email: pubs@thegmcgroup.com, Web: www.gmcpublications.com

Distributed in Australia by Capricorn Link (Australia) Pty Ltd.,
P.O. Box 704, Windsor, NSW 2756 Australia

If you have questions or comments about this book, please contact:
Lark Books
67 Broadway
Asheville, NC 28801
(828) 253-0467
Manufactured in China
All rights reserved
ISBN 1-57990-368-1 (hardcover) 1-57990-673-7 (paperback)

Contents

Introduction

If you have kids, you're bound to have artwork. Maybe, if you're like me, you've got *lots* of artwork. And you probably cherish every piece of it. My collection started over 20 years ago, when my son began doodling with crayons and markers. When a brother appeared, the artwork began to pile up—literally, since I was able to part with very little of it.

When the stacks of folders and shoeboxes began to take over the bedroom, I finally bought large containers and

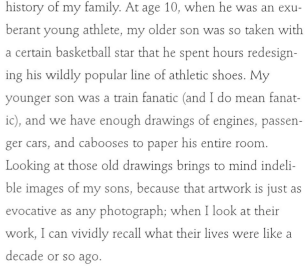

history of my family. At age 10, when he was an exuberant young athlete, my older son was so taken with a certain basketball star that he spent hours redesigning his wildly popular line of athletic shoes. My younger son was a train fanatic (and I do mean fanatic), and we have enough drawings of engines, passenger cars, and cabooses to paper his entire room. Looking at those old drawings brings to mind indelible images of my sons, because that artwork is just as evocative as any photograph; when I look at their work, I can vividly recall what their lives were like a decade or so ago.

Of course, not all of their prodigious output was stored away in the attic. We always displayed some of our favorites in the kitchen art gallery, which also occasionally doubles as our refrigerator. If you have active kids, you've probably learned that the fridge is not the safest spot for these artistic endeavors. Magnets get jarred loose, artwork falls off, the dog walks on it, and or it disappears *under* the

Can we avoid relegating some of the most treasured mementos from our children's lives to the attic?

labeled the trove of drawings, paintings, rubbings, collage, and other assorted creative stuff I'd been hoarding for years.

Actually, the organization of their artwork was a truly delightful chore for me, because it brought back so many memories of my children's lives. To me, their drawings, paintings, and cartoons comprise a visual

refrigerator. Isn't there a better way to preserve and enjoy our children's artwork? Can we avoid relegating some of the most treasured mementos from our children's lives to the attic? Can't we incorporate their creativity into our daily lives?

The answer to those three questions is yes! In the pages that follow, you'll find 39 examples of ways

As you examine the book, you'll see that the projects don't necessarily duplicate the original art precisely. Some use just a single detail from the piece, while others combine elements from several drawings or paintings to create a new form of expression. Once you begin to think about celebrating your children's artwork in your crafting, you'll be amazed at the possibilities that present themselves. Ever thought of using your child's doodles to paint a wainscoting for your home? Look at page 122, and see how easily you can transfer a group of drawings into a decorating

Can't we incorporate their creativity into our daily lives?

to incorporate and transform your children's artwork into craft projects you can proudly use and display in your home. You'll be impressed by the diversity of functional and decorative items included here, all of which are inspired by a piece of children's artwork. The ideas presented here allow you to express your own creativity while you honor your children's artwork; in a very real sense, the projects that you make will be a collaboration with your child, with his or her work as your muse. Look to the sections that follow for advice on how to get started.

marvel. If you've wanted to add some whimsy to your garden, look at the tin ornament on page 86. The charming cup and saucer on page 24 uses a transfer decal material that duplicates the original watercolor in uncanny detail. There are tips in the advice section on page 20 that help you decide on a project, whether you have in mind a specific technique you want to use or a specific piece of artwork you want to incorporate. There's a wealth of ideas to let you take that lonely artwork

7

out of the dingy, dusty attic and give it new life in your home or office.

This book isn't just for parents; it's for anyone who wants to celebrate the creativity of a special child in his or her life. Many of the talented designers who created the projects presented here aren't using artwork from their own children, but that of a granddaughter, a niece, a nephew, or a friend. The crafting processes used are so varied that you're bound to find a project that matches your abilities, and most of them are simple enough that you could learn a new technique, if you're interested in expanding your repertoire of skills. Browse through and see for yourself.

While you're looking through the book, please pay special attention to the wonderful artwork that inspired each project. It's pictured in the book, along with the project created from it. These paintings and drawings were produced by children who love making art, just as yours do. Virtually all of it was conceived during the course of their everyday lives, at home or at school, and was not commissioned to include here. I think you'll get a genuine sense of the young artists' expressions of joy, wonderment, delight, and fascination with the world around them. Take a few moments to appreciate their achievements.

Because we all lead such busy lives, it's doubtful that we can realistically make use of all the creative works we've collected. More importantly, most of the projects included here don't use the original piece of artwork itself, so you'll want to safeguard that special collage that you love so much. And some of the pieces of art that you so admire may be impermanent, too, because of the materials used. Therefore, the book includes sections on the display, storage, and preservation of artwork. If you're the parent of a young child whose artistic career is just beginning, these ideas should keep your collection more manageable than mine was. The section beginning on the next page suggests ways to separate and catalog each of your children's works of art. Then, when you're looking for a drawing to craft with, it will be a snap to examine the possibilities.

Since children tend to make art in inspired bursts, their work has a joy and purity that is irresistible. Keep this premise in mind when you're working—have fun with these projects! This book is designed to be a celebration of the unbridled enthusiasm, spontaneous creativity, and unlimited imagination of the child. It took days to decide on my own projects for the book, because I found so many inspiring pieces in those boxes in the attic. You, too, will be joyfully overwhelmed at the possibilities presented to you when you make a craft from your child's artwork. Enjoy the process, and savor the memories that those paintings of flowers, sketches of dinosaurs, and drawings of baby brother bring back to you. Cherish the memories and the artwork, for both are precious.

Organization, Preservation, and Storage

Before you begin to craft with your child's artwork, take a moment to reflect on the importance of your crayon and marker masterpieces. Then, decide how to store and organize your collection while you plan a project or two (or three).

DOES IT MATTER WHAT IT MEANS?

When you look at a piece of your child's artwork, what do you see? A rainbow, or a moment in time when your child was happy and carefree? When psychologists and psychiatrists consider the meaning of children's art, they discuss its importance as a measure of a child's development and emotional well-being. When my son was drawing sneakers, did he wish to become as famous as that basketball star he admired? Probably so. When his younger brother painted a train steaming through the countryside, was he hoping for a life of adventure and travel?

Maybe. But these right-brained expressions are simply a visual representation of their youthful interests; in layperson's terms, my kids simply enjoyed drawing things they liked. And these are the pieces that I admire and appreciate; to me, all of their output is art of the highest form.

So, look for both things in your child's drawing: Gosh, that is a really beautiful rainbow, and I'll bet she was really happy when she drew that. This book honors children's artwork, from the simple scribble to the elaborate oil painting, and everything in between. It presents you with many, many ways to use your own creativity to make craft projects based on those special pieces of art, and you'll be able to appreciate them every day.

Most children need little encouragement to draw or paint. In early childhood, drawing is recognized as a form of communication before the development of the more complex skills of reading and writing. In fact, much of what is so charming about kids' art is its simplicity and spontaneity. One of the designers who contributed several projects to this book wrote, "I love children's art; it's pure and from the heart." Many famous artists shared this view, too. Pablo Picasso has often been quoted as saying that, while he learned to paint like one

When his younger brother painted a train steaming through the countryside, was he hoping for a life of adventure and travel?

of the masters in only four years, it took him a lifetime to learn to paint like a child. He also expressed his belief that every child was an artist. In fact, Picasso was one of several renowned artists who were collectors of children's art.

Will your child become a Matisse or an O'Keefe? Probably not. But that shouldn't diminish the significance of her expression and its importance to you. For example, the platter on page 76 was based on a piece of artwork that a young girl drew for her brother's birthday; now, it's been transformed into an item that the family can use again and again on special occasions. You may choose to make a project because the piece of artwork is meaningful, because it's appealing, or maybe just because it's silly and fun; take a look at the apron on page 32, with its collection of smiling faces. So, it's time to get started. Let's begin with organizing the artwork while you're deciding on a project.

ORGANIZATION

Heed this advice from an experienced collector of children's art—start organizing the pieces that you want to save *now*. Only you can decide what's worth keeping (I probably agonized over everything I tossed away), but make the commitment to organize it as you accumulate it. Then, you won't have to hunt through shoeboxes to find the pieces you want to use in craft projects.

Office supply centers offer some quick and easy solutions if you're overwhelmed with sketches and watercolors, for they stock a great variety of files and folders with features that make them distinctive and perfect to store art. Look for expanding files with a display window; you can insert a piece of your child's art as an identifying "tag." You can purchase brightly colored file folders and key the color to the child's grade or age; then store these in a file cabinet. For large pieces, consider a slim portfolio, labeled appropriately, that can be stored flat or slipped in behind furniture; these can be made easily at home, too, with poster board or mat board. Mailing tubes are a wonderful space-saving way of storing lots of art, particularly if your child likes to work on larger paper; recycled blueprint or poster tubes work well for this purpose, too. Don't forget to label them with the child's name and age; he'll probably be more than happy to help you decorate his portfolio or tube. Browse through an office supply center for an hour or two and you'll find many

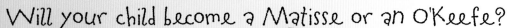

Will your child become a Matisse or an O'Keefe?

items to help you organize your child's work. These are all good temporary fixes, but for more permanent storage ideas, read on.

PRESERVATION

Many of these items mentioned above won't be of *archival* quality, meaning that their components are pH neutral—neither acidic nor alkaline. Many papers and paper products, particularly those made from wood pulp, are acidic and will eventually damage anything else that they touch. In fact, the acidity of paper actually increases with age, and this is what makes paper brown and brittle over time. Vinyls are also harmful—and the old magnetic photo albums that so many of us used for our baby pictures are actually causing our memories to deteriorate.

Now, that said, one of the designers in this book used a piece of his artwork that his mother saved—over 40 years ago! Look at the pieces in the photo below;

though the paper has browned, the pieces of artwork are in relatively good shape. Most assuredly, they weren't created on acid-free paper, with acid-free inks, and stored in an acid-free container. But you should consider this information on preservation, because if you're the parent of a young child, you can shop for archival art supplies and store your child's finished pieces more carefully than we did in the past. (I'd be

A VARIETY OF FILES, FOLDERS, AND MAILING TUBES CAN BE A GREAT HELP IN ORGANIZING YOUR COLLECTION OF ARTWORK. ACID-FREE MATERIALS PROVIDE THE GREATEST PROTECTION FOR YOUR MASTERPIECES.

NOTE THE EFFECTS OF AGING SHOWN HERE; THE PIECES OF ART AT THE RIGHT WERE CREATED ALMOST 50 YEARS BEFORE THE PIECES ON THE LEFT.

PRESERVATION MATERIALS

I f you're interested in preserving some existing artwork created on paper, here are some items that you may want to investigate. Specialty archival suppliers, scrapbooking stores, craft stores, and art supply shops are sources for these products. If you don't have an archival supplier near you, one's just a mouse click away on the Internet. Most of the page protectors, sleeves, and bags are made from "poly" products—polypropylene, polyethylene, and polyester film.

Sleeves and page protectors—*Clear protection for artwork, available in a number of shapes and sizes. You can find a variety of these at a local craft store or office supply shop, but if you need to protect an oversized document, look to an archival supplier.*

Bags—*Great for bulky or slightly oversized documents; you can enclose an entire box in some of these bags. Others are large enough for a matted print. You can also get hanging file bags that are clear, a great advantage when you're trying to locate a piece of artwork.*

Folders and boxes—*Available in manuscript size and larger, some are made of fabric and acid-free paper and constructed with neutral adhesives. Folders range from letter to map size. Archival board is also on the market, if you want to build your own box.*

Albums and scrapbooks—*Great for storing letter-sized pieces of artwork.*

pH pens—*Not for writing or drawing, but to test the pH of materials. These are useful for checking the acidity of drawings that come home from school, for instance, so you can determine how to best store and preserve them.*

Silica gel packages—*Don't have a truly dry space in your home, or no storage space available where it is truly dry? These packages of silica gel, a drying agent, can help protect your artwork when it's in a storage container. (This is the same stuff that comes in the box with your new pair of sneakers.)*

Metal cabinets—*If money were no object, you could buy a commercial quality document cabinet for flat storage of artwork.*

willing to bet that my shoebox portfolio wasn't archival quality.) And really, my collection is faring pretty well considering its rude treatment over the years. Still, if you want the very best protection for your artwork, store it in the acid-free items that are available; see the chart above for information on these products.

But, here's the catch: If it's on paper, your artwork itself is probably acidic. Yikes! All the more reason to preserve the artwork in a craft project, right? Fortunately, there are a number of products available to help solve this problem and safeguard your collection if you're really worried about its longevity. To preserve a piece of artwork, you can treat any paper-based product with a commercial deacidification

dry, dark place to store the artwork, because light and heat intensify the chemical decomposition of paper. Watercolors, too, are particularly sensitive to light, so keep that in mind if you have a young painter at home.

Since much of your kid's artwork may come home from school, you'll often find paper clips, rubber bands, staples, cellophane tape, or self-adhesive notes attached. Remove these things right away, because you don't want to store the art with any of these articles remaining on the paper. They, too, can be damaging to the longevity of your original pieces.

spray to neutralize and protect it.

Although you can also make your own neutralizing solution, it can't be used on items that have water-soluble inks on them, because the neutralizing solution is also a water-based product. So if you've just got to have those purple file folders from the office supply store, go ahead and buy them to organize your kids' artwork; if you treat the folders, they'll be much safer to use. But don't be consumed by worrying about the artwork decaying; if you store it safely in a dry place, it wll probably be fine for your lifetime.

Just as there are products to safeguard existing paper products, there are now a number of art supplies you can buy that are already of archival quality, including various types of paper, ink, and adhesives. See the chart on page 14 for more information on these items.

STORAGE

If you've got artwork in the attic or the basement, consider moving it. (Okay, I confess—my collection's still in the attic. I'm moving it tomorrow.) In all seriousness, the heat and humidity of those spots can be very detrimental to those drawings and paintings you're trying to protect; these are, after all, pieces of your son's or daughter's childhood. Try to find a cool,

WHO INVENTED FINGER PAINTING?

*B*ecause it seems so spontaneous, you might think kids have been dabbing and swirling with their fingers for eons. It is, in fact, a twentieth-century phenomenon.

Ruth Faison Shaw, an American educator, art therapist, and artist born in Kernersville, North Carolina, developed both the technique and the medium. While a young teacher in Rome, she was inspired by the sight of a student drawing on the wall while he had iodine on his finger. Afterward, she spent many months of research and experimentation to develop a safe, nontoxic formula that children could use on their hands, finally patenting her product in 1931.

Later, Shaw made major contributions to the field of art therapy, using finger painting as a tool.

ARCHIVAL ART SUPPLIES

Thanks to the popularity of scrapbooking, there are now numerous supplies on the market that are archival quality and acid-free. Remember that every item that touches the artwork, including inks and adhesives, must also be archival or the acid will migrate throughout the piece. Look for these items in a craft store, a scrapbooking specialty store, an art supply shop, or even office supply centers, which generally have some archival materials. Before you purchase anything, check the label to make sure that it says "acid-free."

Paper—*Either the acid has been buffered or the paper is manufactured from a non-wood source, like cotton. The selection now is mind-boggling, including everything from copy paper to that old standby, construction paper. Watercolor paper, sketchbooks, and drawing pads can all be made of acid-free materials. Cards and envelopes can also be found.*

Canvas—*Both archival-quality pads and artist's canvas are available.*

Inks—*An amazing assortment of pens, markers, and stamp pads are on the market, most all of them kid-friendly. For permanence, also choose those that are waterproof. You can even buy archival pens that make fantastic dots or pens designed for stenciling.*

Adhesives—*In liquid form, double-sided tape products, and now spray, too. If your child likes to collage, look for these archival materials, because they come in really fun formats, like glue dots, glue and tape pens, and glue sticks.*

Assorted interesting stuff—*Chalk, pencils, dimensional lacquer, and stickers. For the latter, look to a scrapbooking source.*

Got a computer? If you also have a scanner, you could catalog and store the pieces you choose on your hard drive or burn them onto discs for storage.

A digital camera will work for this archiving function, too. But to use these electronic methods, you'll need a computer with lots of memory, speed, and storage space to handle the information from a high-resolution scan, which is how you should store the images of your child's artwork. Likewise, you'll want a high-resolution digital camera, particularly if you plan to print out the images later. Most of the economical digital cameras are designed for Internet use, to create

email attachments or imagery for websites. The acceptable resolution for the screen is much lower than acceptable print resolution.

Here's yet another way the computer can help you catalog your daughter's artwork. If you find that she's interested in the computer, as most kids are, encourage her to learn to draw electronically and save her creations. There are some really simple draw programs she can begin with, but children now have such an affinity for the computer that she'll probably quickly outgrow it. More advanced graphics programs offer infinite possibilities for digital drawing.

Display Ideas

Since it's already been decided that you can probably never craft with your entire collection of kids' artwork (even if you lived to be 100), no doubt you'll want to keep some on exhibit at home before you think about storing it. There's just no way you can take that smiling bug with the green eyes and put it away yet! A few of our favorite pictures are still out after many years, and I resurrected one special piece during my research for this book. If you have a particularly rowdy household, consider color copying all of the artwork that you hold dear and storing the originals. If an errant tennis ball knocks your copied artwork into the aquarium, you'll still have the original secreted away.

A home display can be helpful, too, while trying to decide which pieces to incorporate into projects. Take your time and consider the possibilities at your leisure.

If you have a particularly rowdy household, consider color copying all of the artwork that you hold dear and storing the originals.

HERE ARE TWO EASY DISPLAY IDEAS; ALL YOU NEED FOR THE ONE AT LEFT IS CLOTHESLINE AND SOME BRIGHTLY PAINTED CLOTHESPINS. THE DISPLAY AT THE RIGHT, WITH A ROD AND HOOKS, CAN BE CHANGED QUICKLY TO ACCOMMODATE A YOUNG ARTIST'S NEW WORKS.

IS CONSTRUCTION PAPER JUST FOR KIDS?

O*f course not! But your collection of artwork is bound to include a piece or two of this sturdy paper made from wood pulp. You may see it referred to as "classroom art paper," because this colorful, all-purpose material is used for drawing, painting, folding, and well, constructing things.*

Famous artists have also used such papers in their works, including Marc Chagall and Jackson Pollack. And if your child has ever created cut-outs from construction paper, he's in good company: Henri Matisse, one of the most influential painters of the last century, created papercuts toward the end of his life, when he was unable to stand at the easel. These collages are considered among his finest artistic achievements.

Your child will get a kick out of seeing his artwork on display at home, too, and of course you'll enjoy looking at it every day, so here are some ideas about exhibiting the pieces.

INFORMAL DISPLAYS

Most of these suggestions allow you to update the artwork in a jiffy, so the drawings in them can be switched and swapped. Several of these are quick, easy, and inexpensive to install, but there's information about framing and placement in the next section, if you want to go a more formal route.

—CLOTHESLINE AND CLOTHESPINS. Can it get any easier? All you need is a little space to string the line, and add some colorful plastic clothespins or paint some wooden ones yourself. This casual idea is good for a family room or a child's room, strung at about eye level; for a more sophisticated look, use wire and stainless steel supports.

—PEGBOARD. This is an adaptation of the previous idea. Place lengths of clothesline along a piece of pegboard, securing the line at the edges, to form a "ladder" of artwork. Vary the angles, if you want. Use clothespins or funky, coated paper clips to secure the pieces.

—CLIPBOARDS. Look for fluorescent ones at the office supply store, or go for the traditional look; hang a group of a half-dozen or so randomly, overlapping slightly, if desired. You can mix sizes, too, for the artist who works in different media—a sheet of

A GROUP OF UTILITARIAN (AND INEXPENSIVE) CLIPBOARDS CAN BECOME A GALLERY IN YOUR HOME. MIX AND MATCH BRIGHT COLORS FOR A PLAYFUL DISPLAY.

notebook paper today, an index card tomorrow.

—MEMORY BOARD. Make these with ribbon, decorative string, or twine crisscrossed over a base; look for one that is ready-made, too. These can double as a family message center; see the great project on page 105 for another take on this idea.

—BOOKCASES. If you're lucky enough to have built-in bookcases in your home, you can designate a shelf or two for family art exhibits. To use this space to hang art, use eyebolts, steel cable, and clamps to make a contemporary display.

—DISPLAY SHELF. Here's a great idea for the kitchen or family room: install a shelf near the ceiling and use it for exhibition space. You can place dimensional items on top, too, and tack pieces to the bottom, if you need to.

—ROD AND BRACKETS. Take these basic materials, add a few shower curtain rings and clips, and you've got a quick and easy display. Add some additional decorative elements, like the seasonal embellishments shown in the photo on page 15, for a festive arrangement.

—GARDEN BORDER FENCING. Tack this right onto a wall, maybe a strip or two, and use clothespins to secure the artwork. If you're into salvage, you may find some antique fencing that would be wonderful.

—MAGNETIC BULLETIN BOARDS. Buy several, hang them as a grouping, and use these as a canvas for your favorite drawings or paintings. Find some great magnets, colorful magnetic clips, or magnetized bulldog clips to attach your artwork.

—EASEL. About as simple as it gets! Look for an easel to display favorite pieces, whether they touch your heart or tickle your funny bone. Move the easel around the house, too.

FORMAL DISPLAYS

If your child produces some really imaginative and creative work, you may want to mount it on stretchers or frame it. If she's particularly prolific, you may even want to take a course in framing to learn to do it yourself. Whether you do your own framing or have a professional do it for you, make sure your piece will

DO YOU HAVE A BUSY PAINTER AT HOME? MAYBE YOU'LL WANT TO MOUNT AND FRAME HER WORK.

be done with acid-free components. Here are several considerations when you frame children's art:

—MAT. When you're choosing a mat for your artwork, remember that you want to draw attention to the piece itself, not the mat. Generally speaking, look for a mat that is the same or a similar color as the predominant hue in the artwork, or even lighter if you want the artwork to be more noticeable. A darker mat can be overpowering. A large mat can make a small piece seem more important, while a small mat can make a large piece look more prominent. Oil paintings are rarely matted.

—FRAME. The frame itself should enhance your artwork, and you have some choices about whether you want to set off a piece with a truly distinctive frame or have the frame barely noticeable by blending it with some element of your chosen painting or draw-

ing. Let your child's art be the guide. Keep in mind that wood is acidic (you probably know this by now), so professional framers apply a coat of sealer or polyester tape to the portion of the frame that actually touches the artwork. Metal frames are not acidic, so these are used for most museum-quality conservation.

—ARRANGEMENT. Your personal taste will probably dictate how you arrange the artwork. If you have a traditional home, you may opt for a symmetrical arrangement of identically framed pieces; if your home is contemporary, you might want an informal grouping of pieces in different sizes and types of frames.

—PLACEMENT. So, where you will hang your treasures? I often dream of filling my long downstairs hallway with a collection of copies of family photographs that I have scanned and archived in the computer (that's another book). But, my point is, you may have a similar space in your home that is underutilized, and it may make a perfect home gallery. In fact, hanging art in a hallway frees you from having to relate it to your furnishings, and you can use the framed pieces almost like wall covering, hanging things high and low.

—EASEL SYSTEM. If you have an accomplished painter, you'll surely want to display these works to their best advantage. Consider installing an easel system, similar to those you would see in an art gallery. These have sliding brackets that allow you to hang multiple works on a central, stationary pole mounted to your wall. The construction allows for easy display changes. There are also hybrids of this system that are designed to exhibit magazines; these, too, could probably be adapted to use for children's artwork.

COLLECTIONS
OF CHILDREN'S ART

There are many outstanding collections of kids' art throughout the world, with museums dedicated to collecting and exhibiting the artwork of children. Of course, there are numerous hands-on museums and exhibitions designed to encourage creativity and artistic expression in children. Your local hospital, airport, or bank may even have some works on display. Here are some interesting tidbits about collectors, collections, and exhibitions of children's art.

Frances Derham, an Australian teacher and artist, collected children's art for over 50 years. Her collection, which was donated to her country in 1975 and is housed at the National Gallery of Australia, features works from her native country, Europe, Asia, and the Americas.

In the United States, the Museum of Children's Art in Oakland, California, exhibits only kids' artwork and also supports the arts by offering classes and camps. The Zanesville Art Center in Zanesville, Ohio, has one of the oldest collections of children's art in the country.

Over 300 school students from Glasgow, Scotland, participated in a three-year project to record and interpret the city's architecture. The final product was a 3,000-square-foot painting of a child's view of Glasgow. Over a quarter million people attended the exhibition.

In Great Britain, the London International Gallery of Children's Art is devoted to the artwork created by children all over the world.

Web-based collections of children's art abound, some with international collections and others that accept submissions of kids' artwork. A quick search on the Internet will yield a number of these sites. There are several organizations devoted to the study of children's art.

The United Nations Children's Fund, commonly known as UNICEF, has a vast archive of international children's art. The organization's popular cards, which have often featured this artwork, support its activities for child advocacy. UNICEF's first card, produced in 1949, was based on a watercolor painting that the organization received from a seven-year-old Czech girl; she was expressing her thanks for the help her village received following World War II.

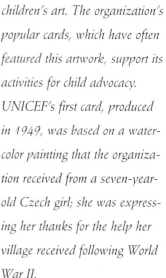

MADISON MAI TRIMBLE. FINGER PAINT AND WATERCOLOR ON PAPER. 6½ x 4½ INCHES (16.5 x 11.4 CM). 2000.

Crafting Advice

When you're planning a project based on a piece of artwork, you can approach the process from a couple of different perspectives. Since you'll be using pieces from your own collection, and won't be using the same artwork as the designers in this book, look to their projects for inspiration as well as technical information.

CHOOSING ARTWORK

If you know you'd like to do a silk painting, for instance, the pillow on page 96 offers practical direction, with instructions that describe the important steps in the process. Then, match a piece of artwork to that technique. Conversely, if you see a project you love, figure out which of your pieces is best suited to create a similar one. For example, if you'd like to feature the artwork of several of your children in the same project, consider the calendar on page 39. Finally, if you've already decided on a piece of artwork to use, browse through the projects to find an idea that inspires you.

Although there are a variety of craft processes in the book, there's bound to be one that's just right for your interests and skills—whether you saw, stamp, sew, paint, decoupage, or transfer. Designers who created projects for this book worked with tin, aluminum, wood, silk, cotton, yarn, gourds, glass, paper, and soap. There are objects just for fun, like a doll; items

Sometimes the subject matter of the artwork seems to suggest a good project.

you can use every day, like a key pegboard; and projects to decorate your home, like a table runner. If you've never embroidered before but have always wanted to learn, look at the linens project. The gourd and the wall hanging are good suggestions for items that your child can help you make.

Sometimes the subject matter of the artwork seems to suggest a good project; the farm drawings made the perfect embellishment for the picnic tablecloth on page 116. Likewise, a pair of abstract paintings only need to be transferred to canvas to become pieces of fine art. Look at these on page 100; framed or unframed, they're fit for a gallery.

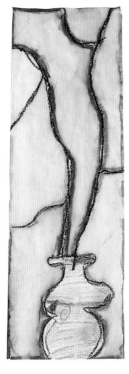

For the most part, copies of the artwork are used in these projects, so you can store your originals for posterity; a notable exception is the beautiful extension painting on page 120. Practically none of the artwork incorporated into the projects presented here was created specifically for this book; in other words, the designers of the projects used pieces from their own collection. If you wanted, you could certainly ask your child to draw bugs, bananas, or bears to use in your crafting as you see fit.

An office supply center and a full-service copy shop can provide many services to help you craft with kids' artwork. They can collate, bind, copy, print, pad, lam-

In the photo above, notice how the original artwork seems to really look like stained glass, which is the project inspired by the painting. Consider all the possibilities while you plan. Enjoy the process of searching through your collection, finding a piece that you love, and creating a new project with it. But if your daughter comes home from school tomorrow with a wonderfully whimsical painting, start right away.

DESIGN CONSIDERATIONS

When you look through the projects, notice that some designers used a very literal interpretation of the work, while others took only a detail or two to use in a project. Still others combined motifs from several works. Change a color, remove a line, or add a detail if you want—set your own imagination free. Don't let the project overshadow the artwork you want to showcase, though; a favorite pencil drawing might get lost on a busy background, for example.

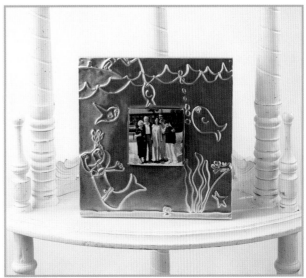

THE DESIGNER OF THIS PROJECT COMBINED MOTIFS FROM SEVERAL DIFFERENT DRAWINGS TO CREATE THIS CHARMING FRAME.

inate, and even design for you at very reasonable prices, if you need a little help with some aspect of a project. I also used the services of a professional digital imaging shop to create a project, and the cost was quite reasonable. If you have a really great idea but don't have the skills or equipment to create it, don't be deterred. See what resources are available in your community.

COLOR COPYING AND COLOR LASER PRINTS ARE COMBINED IN THIS PROJECT; THE ORIGINAL ARTWORK AND A COLOR COPY ARE SHOWN AT LEFT. ELEMENTS FROM THE COLOR COPIES ARE GLUED ONTO A TEMPLATE CREATED ON THE COMPUTER, SHOWN AT RIGHT. SEE THE FINISHED PROJECT ON PAGE 44.

DO YOU KNOW HOW TO MAKE A CRAYON?

Everybody knows that the crayon is the staple of every kid's collection of art supplies. But do you know how they're made?

Traditional crayons are made from paraffin wax and pigment. The ingredients are heated until they reach a liquid state, and the liquid crayons are poured into a heated mold. The crayon forms are cooled with water—they're ready in less than 10 minutes! One leading manufacturer makes over 2 million crayons every day. You can also buy earth-friendly crayons made from soybean oil.

Unfortunately, no matter how much you love a drawing, sometimes it just might not translate well to the crafting process; in that case, just frame it and keep it on display as is. Or, you may want to polish a new skill before you attempt a project—I want to create a mola, a reverse-applique wall hanging based on the Central American technique, but my needlework skills need some improvement. I'll store my charming construction paper collage until I've practiced a bit more.

PRACTICAL STUFF

There are three categories of projects in the book: Functional and Fun (items to use); Festive and Fabulous (things for celebrations); and Decorative and Dazzling (objects for your home). Most of the instructions for the projects that follow assume a few things—first, and most important, that you have the artwork that you're going to incorporate. Therefore, this item isn't listed in the What You Need list. Second, the directions presume that you'll make all needed copies yourself. Of course, you can have professionals at a copy shop make these for you, too, if you'd rather. Since most of us don't have laminating equipment at home, we figure you'll have that service provided for you. The instructions are thorough, and tips and alternatives are provided for nearly every project if you want a few more ideas.

Finally, here are some suggestions to make crafting with your kid's artwork easier and cheaper.

—COLOR COPYING. The quality of a color copy can be astounding, and they're marvelous for the crafter. However, they're relatively expensive, so if you're using a self-service copier, be sure you understand how to operate the machine. Ask first, because you'll probably have to pay for all the copies you make, whether they're usable or not. Get a quick lesson before you start.

—COLOR LASER PRINTING. I don't have a pricey laser printer at home, so I go to my full-service copy shop and use the design station there when I need to scan and print for projects. Color laser prints are very expensive, so it's worth your while to print a black-and-white copy first, if you're doing a project like the wrapping paper on page 82. Check this copy for placement, and then print the color version when you are satisfied with your design. Since color laser prints are even more expensive than color copies, make multiples on the copy machine, not the laser printer.

—FABRIC TRANSFERS. Though you can buy these materials for printers or copiers, many professional copy shops won't let you use them in their machines, or they may restrict their use to their own brand of transfer paper. Be sure to investigate these methods thoroughly before you invest in the supplies.

WHEN YOU'RE CHOOSING PIECES OF ARTWORK FOR A PROJECT, IT MAY HELP TO TACK THEM UP AND STUDY THEM DURING YOUR PLANNING PROCESS.

Projects I

func·tion·al

adj. Serving a useful purpose.

+

fun *n.* Amusing, playful, or enjoyable activity.

"The great man is he who does not lose his child's heart."
Mencius, philosopher, 372-289 B.C.

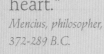

Flowery Cup + Saucer

ARTIST
Jaime Snyder

PROJECT DESIGNER
Suzanne Tourtillott

The only thing lovelier than this cup and saucer is the original artwork that inspired it. Though the pieces appear to have been painted, they were in fact decorated with a transfer material.

JAIME SYNDER. INK AND WATERCOLOR ON PAPER.
11 X 14 INCHES (27.9 X 35.6 CM). 2001.

What You Need

Large cup and saucer, with a diameter of about 4 inches (10.1 cm)

Cloth tape measure

Bleach and water

Color photocopier

Water-slide decal transfer paper

Scissors

Small, shallow tray or dish with plain water

Small squeegee

Craft knife

Paper towel (if necessary)

What You Do

1 Beginning at one side of the handle, use a tape measure to find the circumference and height of the cup. The usable area of this cup measured 12 x 4 inches (30.5 x 10.1 cm). To remove any soap or oily residue, briefly soak the ceramic pieces in water with a small amount of bleach, and let them dry.

2 Measure the dimensions of the artwork, then calculate how much it will need to be reduced or enlarged to fill the cup's area. The size of the artwork shouldn't exceed the smaller of the cup's dimensions. (The flowers and stems of this original artwork measured 8 x 6 inches [20.3 x 15.2 cm]; they were reduced by 50 percent, to 4 x 3 inches [10.1 x 7.6 cm]). This allowed the design to be repeated three times around the cup. If you choose to embellish the saucer, make additional copies at the appropriate size.

3 Photocopy the original artwork onto the water-slide transfer paper. Follow the manufacturer's instructions for fusing the copy's toners.

4 Use very sharp scissors to trim closely around the images, leaving only a small margin. Cut small notches at curve points to allow the decal to be adjusted as necessary to fit the curve of the cup's surface.

5 Submerge a cutout decal in a shallow tray or dish of plain tap water until it floats free of its backing material, usually about one minute. Soak each decal only when you're ready to apply it.

6 Transfer the decal to the cup's surface. Use the squeegee to gently work air bubbles from the center of the decal out to its edges. It's important that the decal be in full contact with the ceramic piece's surface, so work under a good light, watching for the smallest bubbles. Use the craft knife to cut additional tiny notches at the edges so the decal follows the curves. Do the final smoothing with your finger or a dampened soft paper towel. The decal material becomes brittle as it dries, so treat it gently.

7 Follow the manufacturer's instructions to fuse the decal to the ceramic surface. For example, the pieces in this project were placed in a 150°F (66°C) oven for 10 minutes, then the temperature was increased 50°F (10°C) every 10 minutes thereafter, to bake at a top temperature of 350°F (177°C) for 10 minutes. Turn off the oven. Let the pieces cool in the opened oven, since the decals may be fragile.

Artsy Soap

ARTISTS:
Thomas Goodwin & Olivia Maddix

PROJECT DESIGNER:
Allison Chandler Smith

These delightful soaps are certain to bring a smile. This is an excellent project for preschooler art, because the true charm of that work is its simplicity. Keep these bubbly bars on display to brighten your day.

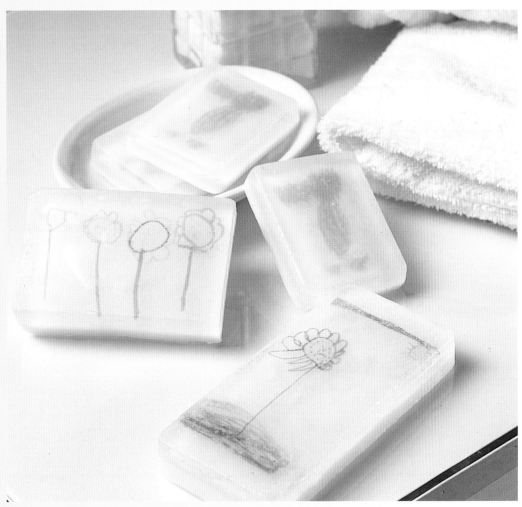

**THOMAS GOODWIN. CRAYON ON PAPER.
5 X 8 INCHES (12.7 X 20.3 CM). 2002.**

**OLIVIA MADDIX. CRAYON AND MARKER ON
PAPER. 6 X 4 INCHES (15.2 X 10.2 CM). 2002.**

What You Need

Color photocopier

Transparency sheet

Scissors

Clear glycerin melt-and-pour soap

Sharp knife

Glass measuring cup

Microwave oven

Soap molds (or small plastic containers)

Opaque glycerin melt-and-pour soap

Cooking spray

Rubbing alcohol in a small spray bottle

What You Do

1 Use the color copier to transfer the original artwork onto a sheet of transparency, reducing or
enlarging it as needed. Cut out the images, leaving a
small, even border around each.

2 Cut the clear glycerin into small chunks with the
knife. Place about $^1/_3$ cup (90 ml) of glycerin
chunks into the glass measuring cup. Melt it in the
microwave oven, following the manufacturer's
instructions. Do not overheat.

3 Spray the mold with cooking spray. Pour a $^1/_2$-inch
(1.3 cm) layer of melted soap into the mold.
Allow it to cool until a thin, solid layer forms across
the top. Spritz with a fine mist of alcohol. Now, gently place the copied artwork facedown on the top of
the layer of soap.

4 Cut the opaque glycerin into small chunks. Melt
about $^1/_3$ cup (90 ml) in the measuring cup as in
step 2. Again, avoiding overheating the soap.

5 Pour a $^1/_2$-inch (1.3 cm) layer of the opaque glycerin on top of the first. Allow the soaps to cool
completely before removing them from the molds.

Striped Floorcloth

ARTIST:
Devon Dickerson

PROJECT DESIGNER:
Allison Chandler Smith

If you need to brighten up a dull corner of your home, here is the project for you. This floorcloth teeming with turtles was designed to showcase a collection of colorful drawings. Don't hesitate to tromp all over it!

DEVON DICKERSON. MARKER ON PAPER.
8½ x 11 INCHES (21.6 x 27.9 CM). 2002.

What You Need

Color photocopier

Scissors

Artist's canvas, cut to your size specifications
   (the finished size here is about 30 x 48 inches
   [76.2 x 121.9 cm])

Latex primer

Foam brushes

Tape measure

Pencil

Blue painter's tape

Credit card or similar burnishing tool

Craft paint in your choice of colors, 3 containers of
   each color

Decoupage medium

Clear acrylic sealer

Double-sided carpet tape, 2 inches (5 cm) wide

What You Do

1 Reduce and copy the art on a color photocopier. Depending on the size of the art, make 15 to 25 copies. Carefully cut the images out, leaving no white background paper on the edges.

2 Paint the canvas with two coats of latex primer.

3 Measure the canvas and mark the spots for the stripes on each end; make them as wide as you wish. This floorcloth has 10 stripes, each 3 inches (7.6 cm) wide. Factor in a 2-inch (2.5 cm) border all around the canvas, so the two outermost stripes will be 5 inches (12.7 cm) wide.

4 Mark each stripe with your chosen paint color; here, each color is used twice. Use the painter's tape to connect the pencil dots so you have a guide to paint every other stripe. You may want to burnish the tape edges with a credit card or similar tool so the paint does not seep underneath.

5 Paint the first set of stripes with two coats of paint in the color marked on the canvas. After the first set of stripes is painted and dry, remove the tape and reposition it to use as a straightedge for the alternate, unpainted canvas stripes. Paint these stripes in the color marked on the canvas, using two coats as before.

6 When the paint is completely dry, attach the photocopied images with a heavy coat of decoupage medium. Allow it to dry, and then paint over the entire image again with the decoupage medium. Next, coat the whole canvas with three or four coats of clear acrylic sealer.

7 Place the canvas wrong side up on a flat surface. Trim each outer edge of the canvas with double-sided carpet tape, leaving the backing on. Cut the corners of the canvas at an angle to miter the edges. Peel off the paper backing, and fold the edges over to finish the floorcloth.

Smiling Apron

ARTIST:
Delaney Mai Trimble

PROJECT DESIGNER:
Dyan Mai Peterson

This designer's granddaughter made her a similar apron that's so cute she can't bear to wear it, so she hangs it in her kitchen as a decoration. She may feel the same way about this light-hearted creation, which is really a breeze to make.

DELANEY MAI TRIMBLE. CONSTRUCTION PAPER COLLAGE: MARKER ON PAPER. 11 x 8½ INCHES (27.9 x 21.6 CM). 1999.

What You Need

Photocopier

Scissors

Transfer paper

Tape

Pencil

Cotton apron (from a craft store)

2 felt-tipped permanent markers, in colors to match the artwork

11 buttons, in colors to complement the artwork

Hot glue gun and glue sticks

What You Do

1 Use a copy machine to reduce or enlarge your image, and make enough patterns to fill the entire apron. This apron has ten smiles in different sizes.

2 Use the scissors to cut out all of the patterns. Place the transfer paper under the patterns and tape them onto the apron.

3 Gently trace each pattern onto the apron. Don't push too hard on the transfer paper, or the dark lines may be difficult to cover with the marker in the next step.

4 Trace over the designs with the marker of your choice, and use a differently colored marker for the bias tape along the border of the apron.

5 Apply the buttons with the hot glue gun, or sew them on, if you prefer.

Tip: Position each pattern at different angles and let them run off the edges for a casual, spontaneous look.

Modernistic Mouse Pad

ARTIST:
Jeremy Shrader

PROJECT DESIGNER:
Valerie Shrader

Every time you check your email and click your mouse, you'll be reminded of your child's imagination. Any type of artwork can be transferred with this technique, and you can trim the foam to the contours of the original piece of art for a unique computer accessory.

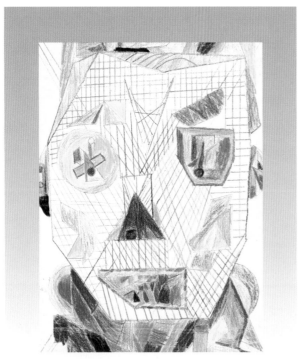

JEREMY SHRADER. COLORED PENCIL AND CRAYON ON PAPER. 9 X 12 INCHES (22.9 X 30.5 CM). 1993.

What You Need

Color photocopier

Black foam sheet

Acid-free spray adhesive

Scissors

Craft knife

What You Do

1 Make a color copy of the original artwork, enlarging or reducing it to approximate the size of a typical 8 x 9 ¼-inch (20.3 x 23.5 cm) mouse pad. You may need to adjust the color settings on the copier to get a true reproduction of the original.

2 Follow the manufacturer's instructions and use the spray adhesive to adhere the copied artwork to one thickness of the foam sheet.

3 Cut out the design, using the scissors or craft knife. If desired, add another thickness of the foam sheet, gluing it to the other layer with the spray adhesive. Cut away the excess foam sheet with the knife or scissors. (Alternatively, you can trace around the design and cut out the second sheet of foam first, and then affix it to the existing mouse pad.)

Tips: You may want to test your mouse on the copied artwork before you make the final project, because some of these devices need a certain type of surface to function properly. The optical mouse can't be used on a white or mirrored surface, while the traditional mouse doesn't function well on a slick surface. However, both types worked perfectly on this unforgettable face.

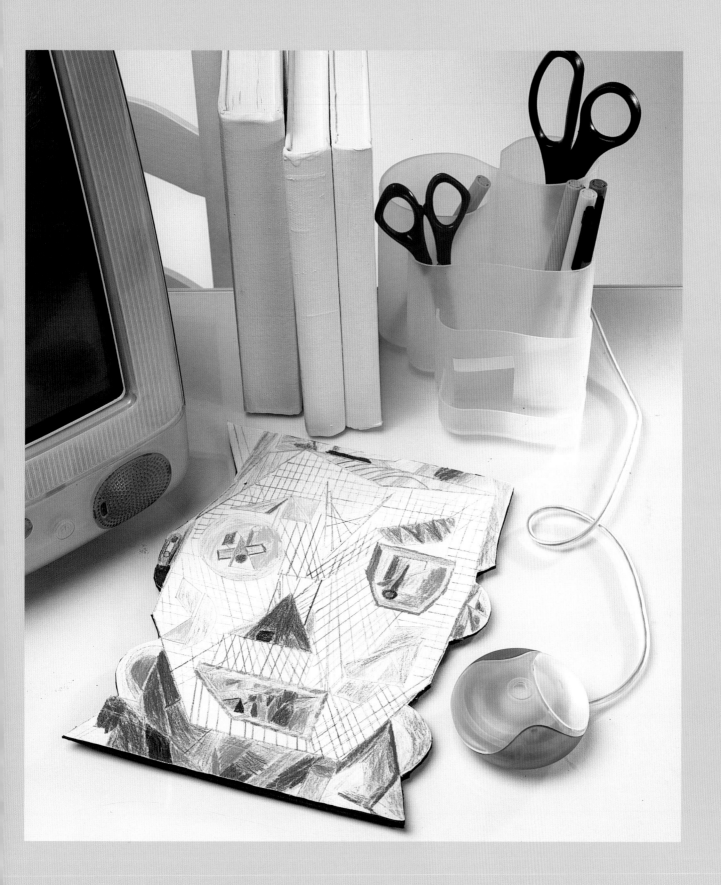

Laminated Luminary

ARTIST:
Corrina Matthews

PROJECT DESIGNER:
Diana Light

This cheerful lantern will brighten any space, indoors or outdoors. The design of this luminary allows you to continually refresh the artwork, because all you have to do is laminate another piece and install the eyelets. Vary the sizes and create distinctive luminaries to showcase the work of each of your children.

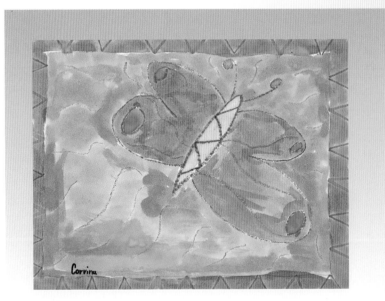

CORRINA MATTHEWS. CRAYON AND WATERCOLOR ON PAPER.
10½ x 8 INCHES (26.7 x 20.3 CM). 2001.

What You Need

Laminated copy of artwork, approximately
14 x 10½ inches (35.6 x 26.7 cm)

Ruler

Pen

Craft knife

Eyelet punch and two 3-mm eyelets

Hammer

5 brass-plated fasteners

Wire cutters

Craft wire

Small pliers, needle-nose and round tip

Template (page 124)

.025 gauge aluminum sheet metal, at least 6 x 21
inches (15.2 x 53.3 cm)

Pencil

Protective gloves

Straight tin snips

Glass votive candleholder, 2 inches (5 cm) in diameter
and 2½ inches (6.4 cm) high

Votive candle

What You Do

1 Have your artwork laminated at a copy shop, leaving a ⅛-inch (3 mm) border around the edges, except for one short side, which needs a ½-inch (1.3 cm) border of laminate. Measure in 3½ inches (8.9 cm) from both outer edges of the artwork, and then make a small mark about ⅜ inch (9.5 mm) from the top of the laminated edge. Use a craft knife to cut small Xs at the marks; this is where you'll install the eyelets for the luminary's handle.

2 Working on a firm, protected surface, use the eyelet punch to install the eyelets at the marked spots.

3 To install the fasteners, mark a series of evenly spaced dots at the short edges of the laminated artwork. Place the dots about ½ inch (1.3 cm) from the sides of the artwork and space them at regular intervals down the sides, starting about ⅝ inch (1.6 cm) from the top. Cut Xs at these marks with a craft knife.

4 Now, bring the sides of the laminated artwork around and overlap them, placing the ½-inch (1.3 cm) border underneath the side with the ⅛-inch (3 mm) border. Push the fasteners through both layers and fasten.

5 To make the handle, use wire cutters to cut about 1 foot (30 cm) of craft wire. Push about 1 inch (2.5 cm) through the eyelet from the inside; hold the wire with the needle-nose pliers and use the round-tip pliers to curl the wire up into a decorative spiral.

6 Place the template from page 124 on the aluminum and trace around it with a pencil. Wear protective gloves as you use the tin snips to carefully cut out the framework for the votive holder.

7 Now, you'll bend each arm of the framework up to create a basket for the glass votive candleholder. Grasp the ends of the long arms about 1 inch (2.5 cm) from the end with the needle-nose pliers, and use the round-tip pliers to make a quarter-turn twist in the arm. Then bend over the ends slightly; this creates the lip to hang the framework from the top edge of the luminary (see figure 1). Place the candle in the holder, insert the holder into the basket, and hang it inside the luminary.

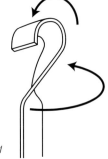

Figure 1

Family Style Calendar

ARTISTS:
Miles Kurzmann & Brooks Wallace

PROJECT DESIGNER:
Corinne Kurzmann

If you have many children, like this designer, here's a fabulous way to showcase artwork from all of them in the same project. Choose the drawings or paintings to correspond with the season, and enjoy searching through your archive of artwork while you're planning.

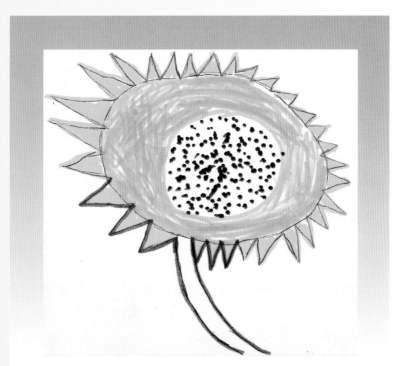

BROOKS WALLACE. MARKER ON PAPER. 11 x 8½ INCHES (27.9 x 21.6 CM). 1997.

What You Need

Color photocopier

Scanner

Computer

Color printer

What You Do

1 After you've selected 12 pieces of artwork, decide on the size of your calendar. The next step is to copy the images or scan the artwork into the computer. If you're copying the images, you'll need to scale them to fit the size you want; this project features pages that are 8½ x 11 inches (21.6 x 27.9 cm). If you work digitally, import the images into your software program and scale to size; you'll probably need lots of available memory to work with these images.

2 You can use a computer program to create a calendar for you, but this one was made in a word processing program with a draw feature. With this method, you can alter the color of the type on the calendar to complement the drawing, as was done here, or even create a unique design each month, with family birthdays or holidays included. Next, print the months of the calendar. Make a cover for the calendar, if desired.

3 Now, collate the calendar, placing the artwork facing the month, with the top of the artwork page facing the bottom of the calendar page. This calendar was created using single-sided copying only, but if you'd rather save some paper and use two-sided copying, you'll need to copy the calendar and the next month's artwork onto the same sheet. For instance, January's calendar and February's art should be copied onto the same sheet of paper.

4 For the best results, take the collated calendar to a copy shop to have it spiral-bound. You can also use a hole punch and ribbon or wire, if you prefer to finish this project at home, but it's quickly and cheaply done at a copy shop.

Tip: If you have more artwork than free time, you can organize the pieces you want to include and have a local full-service copy center create the entire calendar for you.

Alternative: Calendar kits are available for your inkjet printer, complete with the spiral binding. Look for them at an office supply center.

MILES KURZMANN.
WATERCOLOR AND
CRAYON RUBBING ON
PAPER. 11 x 8½
INCHES (27.9 x 21.6
CM). 2001.

BROOKS WALLACE.
WATERCOLOR.
11 x 8½ INCHES
(27.9 x 21.6 CM).
1996.

BROOKS WALLACE.
WATERCOLOR.
11 x 8½ INCHES
(27.9 x 21.6 CM).
1995.

Model T Tray

ARTIST AND PROJECT DESIGNER:
Dana Irwin

This designer kept her childhood sketches of antique cars and used them to create this functional tray that happens to be a lot of fun, too. All it lacks for a great breakfast in bed is pancakes and syrup. Copy and collage your artwork to make this project in a jiffy.

What You Need

Color photocopier

Craft knife or scissors

Tray

Sheet of paper, of a heavier weight than the
photocopies

Acid-free spray adhesive

Sheet of glass, to fit in tray

What You Do

1 Make differently sized copies of the original artwork; make multiples of each size, if desired, as
used in this design.

2 Cut out the images with a craft knife or scissors.

3 Arrange the elements in your collage until you are
satisfied with the design. Then, use the spray
adhesive to glue them to a sheet of paper that's the
same dimensions as the base of the tray; a heavier-
weight paper will be less prone to buckling.

4 After the collage is dry, place it in the tray and put
the glass on top to finish.

Alternative: The tray can also be painted to coordi-
nate with the predominant colors in your artwork, if
desired.

DANA IRWIN. CRAYON AND INK ON PAPER. 11½ X 9 INCHES
(29.2 X 22.9 CM). 1955.

Fall Foliage Notepad

ARTIST:
Dylan Shrader

PROJECT DESIGNER:
Valerie Shrader

Combine computer graphics and color copying to create this useful item for jotting down grocery lists or posting chores. Since you've removed all the artwork from your refrigerator for other projects, you shouldn't have any problem finding a prominent spot for it!

DYLAN SHRADER. CRAYON AND INK ON PAPER. 10½ x 8 INCHES (26.7 x 20.3 CM). 1995.

"Nobody, I think, ought to read poetry, or look at pictures or statues, who cannot find a great deal more in them than the poet or artist has actually expressed."

Nathaniel Hawthorne, writer, 1804-1864

44

What You Need

Scanner

Computer

Graphics software program

Color laser printer

Scissors

Glue stick

Color photocopier

Paper cutter

1 adhesive magnetic sheet, 5 x 8 inches
(12.7 x 20.3 cm)

What You Do

1 Working on an 8½ x 11-inch (21.6 x 27.9 cm) horizontal (landscape) template in your graphics program, create the lines for the pad on only one half of the page. Be sure to leave a margin around each side of about ½ inch (1.3 cm); you may wish to insert a simple graphic shape as a placeholder for the final artwork while you are designing the pad. After you've drawn the lines, change the colors to match those found in the original artwork. Apply the colors randomly.

2 When you're satisfied with the pad template, remove the placeholder and copy and paste the template onto the other side of the page. You should now have two copies of the design on one letter-sized page, as in figure 1; you'll cut them apart later, after you've copied them. Now, print this page onto high-quality laser paper using a color printer.

3 To add the artwork to the pad template, use a color copier to reduce the original to the size desired. Use the scissors to cut out the individual elements you want to feature on the notepad; this pad

has two different designs. The original artwork was actually reduced at two different rates to create the desired size for each leaf used in this project.

4 Glue the elements onto the notepad template and reproduce on a color copier. Make as many copies as desired, and cut them in two with the paper cutter at your copy shop. If you choose more than one design for the pad, alternate them as desired, and collate the sheets to your specifications. Have your copy shop "pad" them along the edge with the adhesive designed for this purpose. Most copy centers will provide this service for a nominal fee.

5 Remove the backing from the magnetic sheet and affix it to the back of the pad.

Alternatives: Just kidding—you don't have to put this on the refrigerator. Omit the magnetic sheet, and it goes to work with you at the office. And, if you're experienced with digital graphics, you can also scan, select, and import the graphic elements into the pad template, rather than using the more traditional cut-and-paste method.

Figure 1. Your notepad template should resemble this drawing when you've completed it.

Phone Book Cover

ARTIST:
Jaime Snyder

PROJECT DESIGNER:
Allison Chandler Smith

These smiling bugs add a touch of whimsy (not to mention beauty) to your poor neglected phone book—since you use the book so often, why shouldn't it look fabulous? Make distinctive borders from linen to frame your art.

47

What You Need

Tape measure

Phone book

Pencil

Paper

Color photocopier

1 yard (.9 m) of decorative burlap

Fabric scissors

Deckle-edged scissors

Linen, in colors that complement your artwork

Pinking shears

Iron-on fabric adhesive

Iron and ironing board

Iron-on flexible vinyl laminate

Fray retardant

Pins and pincushion

Sewing machine

Thread, in colors to match the burlap

"Every genuine work of art
has as much reason for being
as the earth and the sun."

*Ralph Waldo Emerson,
writer and philosopher, 1803-1882*

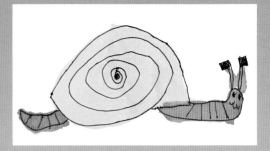

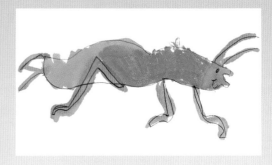

JAIME SNYDER. INK AND WATERCOLOR ON PAPER.
7 x 5 INCHES (17.8 x 12.7 CM). 2002.

What You Do

1 Measure your phone book and decide the size of your artwork. Jot down the figures, because you'll need them again in step 3. Use a color copier to transfer the artwork to the paper, reducing or enlarging as necessary. Make a couple of extra copies, too, for experimentation.

2 To cover a phone book that is $8^{1}/_{2}$ x $10^{3}/_{4}$ x $1^{1}/_{4}$ inches (21.6 x 27.3 x 3.2 cm), cut the burlap to 27 inches (68.6 cm) in length. The length you need will vary depending on the thickness and width of your phone book, so adjust accordingly.

3 Add 1 inch (2.5 cm) to the height measurement from step 1, and cut the burlap to this measurement.

4 Cut the images to the size desired with the deckle-edge scissors, leaving some white space around them. Cut the linen borders to the size desired, using the pinking shears. Follow the manufacturer's instructions and use the fabric adhesive to adhere the images to the linen background. Now, place the images as desired on the right side of the burlap, about $4^{3}/_{4}$ inches (12.1 cm) in from the right edge. (This allowance will create the flap.) Use the fabric adhesive again to adhere the image squares to the burlap.

5 Follow the manufacturer's instructions to affix the vinyl laminate to the burlap; remember to turn the fabric over and iron on the reverse side. Trim the edges and apply the fray retardant.

6 Place the burlap face up on a flat surface. Fold the ends 4 inches (10.2 cm) on each side and pin to make the flaps, wrong sides of the fabric together. Slip the cover over the phone book (tucking the cover and back of the book into the flaps) to make sure that it fits. Make any adjustments as needed.

7 Sew the pockets on both sides in a $^{1}/_{2}$-inch (1.3 cm) seam allowance. Turn the cover right side out, and press gently across the top and bottom, folding the excess fabric under across the top and bottom seam allowance.

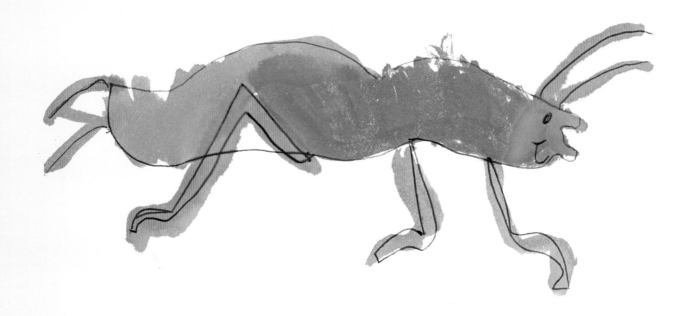

The No. 19 Pegboard

ARTIST:
Dylan Shrader

PROJECT DESIGNER:
Terry Taylor

All aboard! You won't misplace any keys (and be late to the station) when you park them on this locomotive. This artist loved trains when he was young, and this pegboard, which his family will use daily, is a sweet reminder of his boyhood fascination with the mighty machines.

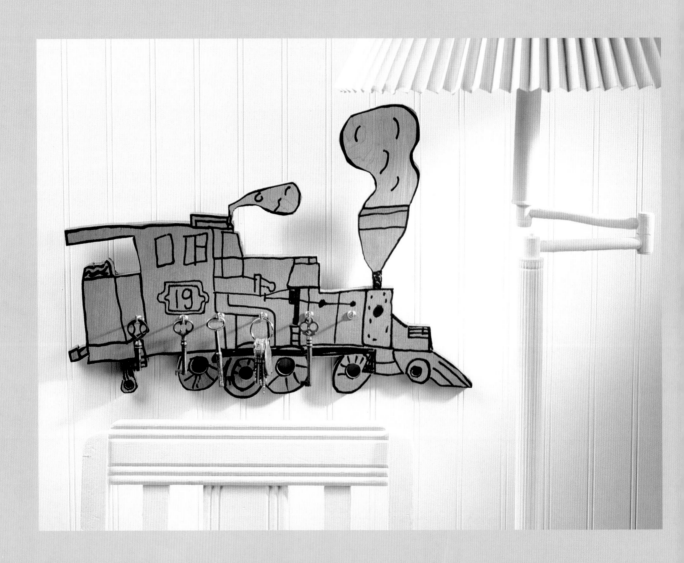

What You Need

Photocopier

1 quarter-sheet of plywood, ½ inch (1.3 cm) thick

Transfer paper

Pencil

Band saw or jigsaw

Sandpaper

Wood stain or acrylic paint, in the color of your
    choice

Paint pen, to match the stain or paints

Picture hanger

Cup hooks

Ruler (optional)

Tip: You no longer have to purchase huge sheets of
plywood. Home improvement centers now stock
small sheets, which is great news for crafters.

What You Do

1 Copy the drawing and enlarge, if necessary.

2 Place the transfer paper on the plywood with the image on top. Trace the image with a pencil, and be sure to include all the features of the original artwork.

3 Cut out the image using a band saw or jigsaw. Sand the edges as needed.

4 Stain or paint the image. Outline and fill in details with the paint pen. Let the image dry thoroughly before proceeding to the next step.

5 Attach the picture hanger to the back.

6 Screw the cup hooks in across the image, placing them by sight or measuring and marking, if necessary.

DYLAN SHRADER. PENCIL ON NOTEBOOK PAPER. 10½ x 8 INCHES
(26.7 x 20.3 CM). 1991.

Intergalactic Lunch Box

ARTIST:
Django Ballentine

PROJECT DESIGNER:
Terry Taylor

You'll be the envy of the office when you carry last night's leftovers in an out-of-this-world lunch box. Choosing a shiny surface for this technique really suits this artwork, with its good-natured astronaut and zooming spacecraft.

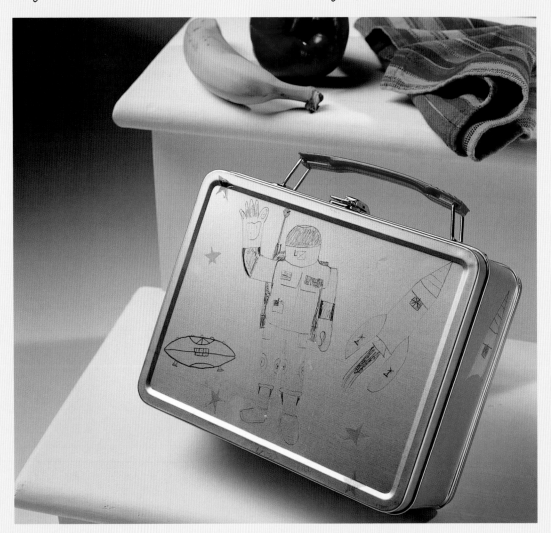

What You Need

Color photocopier

Metal lunch box

Ruler (optional)

Water-slide decal transfer paper

Scissors

Small, shallow tray or dish with water

What You Do

1 Enlarge or reduce the drawing on a color photo-copier. You may want to measure your lunch box first, to make sure that your designs will fit as you envision. Make as many copies as you need to decorate your lunch box.

2 Now, copy the drawing onto the transfer paper; follow the manufacturer's instructions. Use the mirror image option on the copier if you want an exact duplicate of the drawing. Otherwise, just copy the drawing.

3 Cut out the images with the scissors, leaving a small border around the perimeter of each design. Arrange them on the surface of the lunch box as desired.

4 Follow the manufacturer's instructions for applying the decal to the metal surface. For the type of decal paper used here, soak the decal until it floats free of the backing, and then apply it to the lunch box. Smooth out any bubbles. Though the decals can be heat-fused onto the object, this step wasn't used in this project, for fear of melting the handle on the lunch box. It was simply left to air dry, and the process worked perfectly.

Django Ballentine. Metallic pen and ink on paper. 11 x 14 inches (27.9 x 35.6 cm). 2002.

Tip: Water-slide decal transfer paper is available for use in photocopiers and laser printers. Look for it in your local art, craft, or ceramic supply stores, as well as on the Internet.

Heart
Magnetic Message Board

ARTIST:
Brianna Huskey

PROJECT DESIGNER:
Diana Light

Your messages will have special significance on this charming magnetic board—could anyone doubt their heartfelt meaning? Use a complementary piece of artwork for the magnets, if you wish, as this designer did. In a case of welcome serendipity, this tin form was commercially available in the exact shape of the original artwork.

BRIANNA HUSKEY. CRAYON AND MARKER ON PAPER. 8 X 11 INCHES (20.3 X 27.9 CM). 2000.

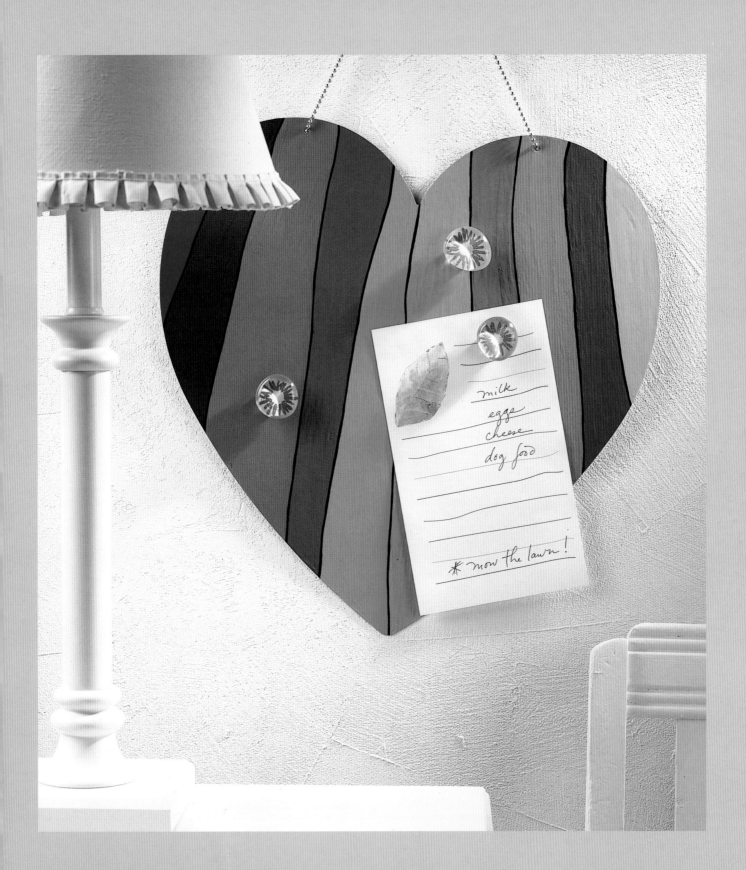

milk
eggs
cheese
dog food

✳ mow the lawn !

What You Need

Tin form with chain

Soap and water

Transfer paper

Pencil or pen

1/2-inch (1.3 cm) flat paintbrush

Glossy acrylic enamel, in colors to match your art
    work

Palette

Plastic wrap (optional)

Black permanent marker (optional)

Clear acrylic enamel spray (optional)

Glass craft stones

Small round paintbrush

Magnets

Cyanoacrylate glue

What You Do

1 Remove the chain from the tin form; clean the form with soap and water, and let it dry. Transfer the drawing to the tin.

2 Use the flat brush to paint the design (in this project, the stripes). If you're using multiple colors, make sure that each section is dry before painting the adjacent section with a new color. Mix any colors as necessary, and cover your palette with plastic wrap to preserve the paints, if you choose; you may want to use some of these colors later on the magnets.

3 After the first coat of paint is dry, go over the design a second time. When this second coat is dry, use the permanent marker to draw in black dividing lines, if appropriate for your design. When the tin is dry, spray with the clear acrylic enamel for added durability, if desired. Allow the clear coat to dry and then reattach the chain.

4 To make the magnet pieces, first wash the craft stones with soap and water, and dry them. They will be decorated using the reverse painting technique, so you'll be working on the backs of the stones.

5 Use the small brush to paint the centers of the flowers, and let dry thoroughly. (In reverse painting, you must let each layer dry completely before adding the next one to avoid ruining the effect.) After the centers of the flowers are dry, paint the petals, and allow the stones to dry. Finally, paint the entire back of the stone with the background color of your choice and let dry.

6 If desired, follow the paint manufacturer's instructions and bake the stones for added durability.

7 After the stones have cooled, glue the magnets to the back. Spray the backs of the magnets with the enamel to prevent leaving marks on the painted surface of the message board.

Alternative: These tin forms are available in several different shapes, so you're sure to find one that suits your artwork.

Picture Sweater

ARTIST:
Micah Pulleyn

PROJECT DESIGNER:
Jeanne Pulleyn

This adorable sweater was knitted by the artist's grandmother, and it's a warm and fuzzy way to honor a special piece of artwork. If you're just learning to knit, you can still create this project by knitting or crocheting the design elements separately and sewing them on.

MICAH PULLEYN. CRAYON ON PAPER. 8 x 10 INCHES (20.3 x 25.4 CM). 1980.

What You Need

Simple sweater pattern (with a simple stitch, such as
   stockinette)

Yarn, in colors to match the original artwork

Knitting needles, in the sizes recommended by your
   pattern

Graph paper or regular paper

Colored pencils

What You Do

1 Transfer the original artwork to graph paper so
you can see which color each stitch should be.
The graph paper should correspond to your knitting
gauge as closely as possible; however, since knitted
stitches aren't perfectly square, you could also draw
your own graph paper to correspond to your stitch
gauge and keep the proportions of the image accurate.
For example, if your knitted gauge was 27 stitches to
4 inches and 38 rows to 4 inches, you would need to
make graph paper that had increments of 27 squares
to 4 inches in width, and 38 squares to 4 inches high.

2 Follow the instructions for the body of your
sweater. To work the picture, use the same weight
yarn as the body of the sweater, because if you
change weight you must add or drop stitches to maintain your gauge. You could easily use a different texture yarn, or use a variety of stitches for texture, as
long as you maintain your gauge.

3 To take more than one color across a row for any
distance, more than five stitches, for instance,
attach another ball of background color on each side.
Use small separate balls of yarn for each color. If you
have to use a color more than once across a row, each
place you use it should have its own ball. Each time

you change colors, be sure to twist the colors around
each other or else you'll leave a hole in your work.

4 Small details are best embroidered on afterwards
in duplicate stitch. If you add any lettering, as in
the project shown here, 5 stitches and 5 rows are the
smallest the letters can be made to be discernible.

Tip: Instead of using balls of yarn for the different
colors in step 3, it may be easier to wind the yarn on
cardboard bobbins and let them dangle on the wrong
side when you're not using them.

Alternative: A fabric appliqué is another way to
transfer a favorite piece of artwork to a garment.

"Imagination, not invention, is the supreme master of art as of life."

Joseph Conrad, writer, 1857-1924

Peerless Postcards

ARTISTS:
Quillan Hunt, Miles Kurzmann, & Brooks Wallace

PROJECT DESIGNER:
Corinne Kurzmann

Need to send a quick note? Make some of these cards on your computer and store the file so you can print them up when you need them. Use this technique to create original party invitations for special events too.

What You Need

Computer

Scanner

Perforated card stock

Printer

Scissors or paper cutter (optional)

Ruler (optional)

Pencil (optional)

What You Do

1 Select the artwork and scan it into the computer. Scale the images to the size desired, and place them into a postcard template in your software program. Use image-editing software, if desired, to tweak the images to your liking.

2 Print your final design onto the perforated postcard stock and separate them carefully. You can also use regular card stock and cut the cards manually; first, use a ruler and pencil to mark the cutting lines.

Alternative: If you make invitations, you can also print out the particulars of your soiree and use two-sided copying to get the image and the invitation onto card stock.

QUILLAN HUNT. CRAYON AND FINGER PAINT
ON PAPER. 8 X 10 INCHES
(20.3 X 25.4 CM). 1997.

MILES KURZMANN. CHALK, CRAYON, AND
WATERCOLOR ON PAPER. 18 X 12 INCHES.
(45.7 X 30.5 CM). 1999.

BROOKS WALLACE. CHALK AND
WATERCOLOR ON PAPER. 18 X 12 INCHES.
(45.7 X 30.5 CM). 1999.

Cockatoo Clock

ARTIST:
Jessica Van Arsdale

PROJECT DESIGNER:
Pamela Paddock

Use this idea as inspiration for making your own fantastical clock, because a drawing or painting of any kind of animal can be adapted for this use. How about a dog dangling the clock from its tail, or a T-rex chomping the timepiece in its ferocious jaws?

JESSICA VAN ARSDALE. OIL ON CANVAS. 11 x 14 INCHES (27.9 x 35.6 CM). 2001.

What You Need

Photocopier

Transfer paper

Pencil

1 quarter-sheet of finish-grade plywood, ½ inch (1.3 cm) thick

Band saw or jigsaw

Fine-grit sandpaper

Wood putty

Drill and assorted drill bits

2 wooden dowels, sized to your drill bit

Hammer

1 tree branch (optional)

Primer

Acrylic paints, in colors to match the artwork

Assorted paintbrushes

1 set of ½-inch (1.3 cm) number stencils

Battery-operated clock mechanism, with a center shaft that will fit through the plywood

Craft wire

Wire cutters

1 package of 19-gauge black wire, at least 8 feet (2.4 m) long (optional)

Scrap piece of lumber, at least 6 x 6 inches (15.2 x 15.2 cm) (optional)

5 finishing nails, ¾ inch (1.9 cm) (optional)

Pliers, needle-nose and regular (optional)

Large black bead (optional)

Wood glue (optional)

1 package of 9- or 10-gauge wire, at least 1 foot (.3 m) (optional)

1 large piece of 90# white artist's vellum (optional)

Craft glue (optional)

What You Do

1 Copy the original artwork, enlarging or reducing to the desired size. Trace the photocopied art onto the ½-inch (1.3 cm) plywood with transfer paper and pencil, and use the band saw or jigsaw to cut out the image. Use the sandpaper to smooth the piece, and fill any imperfections with wood putty. If you do use putty, wait until it's dry and then sand the pieces until smooth.

2 Drill two holes into the bottom of the wooden pattern to attach it to a base (in this project, the branch). Tap the dowels in with the hammer. Drill two corresponding holes on the base with the same drill bit. (This project has two additional holes next to the existing ones for the bird's feet, but you may not need these, depending upon your original artwork.) Paint the front, back, and edges of the wooden image with the primer and the acrylic paints. Let it dry.

3 To make the clock face, use the band saw or jig-saw to cut out a circle from the 1½-inch (1.3 cm) plywood. (In this project, the clock is 5 inches [12.7 cm] in diameter.) Find the center of the wood and drill a hole for the clock mechanism with a ⅝-inch (16 cm) bit. Sand the clock face until smooth, and use wood putty to fill any imperfections. Sand until smooth, if necessary. Prime and paint both sides of the clock face. Let it dry.

4 Next, you'll paint or stencil the numbers on the clock face, approximately ¼ inch (6 mm) from the edge, using the color of your choice. Use an existing clock as an example to determine the placement of the numbers, or better yet, insert the clock mecha-nism and secure it to the face. Start both hands at the 12 o'clock position. Move the minute hand (the

longer of the two) around the dial one revolution until it reaches 12 again; the hour hand will advance to 1 o'clock, 2 o'clock , 3 o'clock, etc. Make a tick mark where the hour hand hits at each successive revolution, and then paint or stencil.

5 Now, attach the clock. Drill a hole through the wooden pattern at the desired location, and drill holes in the clock so you can insert wire and dangle the clock from the image. For this project, twisted craft wire was inserted through the cockatoo's beak and wrapped around a decorative twig, which was then wired to the clock face. Look for a good spot on your wooden creature to hang the clock, and use a little imagination to join the pieces.

6 Although your artwork may not need wire feet, like this cockatoo, these are made from twisted strands of 19-gauge black wire. Two 18-inch (45.7 cm) strands of the twisted wire are looped around five finishing nails; these nails are hammered into scrap wood like the points of a star. Use the needle-nose pliers to curl the feet after each is removed from the

nail template, and insert the feet into the smaller holes next to the dowels in the bottom of the wooden bird.

7 Attach the template to the base by inserting the dowels into the corresponding holes in the base. You may need to sand the dowels down to create a snug fit. For this project, the cockatoo feet are wrapped around the wood with the regular pliers so it looks like the bird is perching on the branch.

8 To add eyes, drill shallow holes where you want to place them, and glue on large black beads. A dab of black paint would do just as nicely!

9 Now, you can adorn your wooden creature with feathers, a shaggy mane, or whiskers, whatever the case may be. Here, pieces of the 9- or 10-gauge wire are cut into varying sizes to provide the structure for the colorful feathers. Rectangles of vellum are folded over the wire, trimmed, and glued together. Then, they're cut and frayed with scissors. Finally, they're painted to match the original artwork. Drill holes where you decide to insert the feature. You may need to glue your embellishments into place if they are dangling below your wooden pattern. This project also has decorative leaves that are cut from the plywood, primed, painted, and connected to the base with branches of twisted craft wire.

Tip: Remember—even though the artwork you want to use for the basis of your clock may be very different than this, these directions give you the basic blueprint for mounting the artwork on a foundation and making and attaching a clock. And then, don't get bogged down in details or anguish over precise measurements with this project; use your imagination on colors and placement of your animal's features. The charm will be in its *imperfection*.

Stylin' Photo Album

ARTIST:
Thomas Taylor

PROJECT DESIGNER:
Terry Taylor

Instead of a traditional (and somewhat boring) cover, this project features a family sketch that is thoroughly twenty-first century. This is a quick, easy, and endearing way to create a truly personal photo album. Guess which brother drew the picture? The one with the cool shades, of course!

What You Need

Photocopier

Crayons

Black felt-tipped pen

Decorative-edged scissors

Black foam sheet

Craft knife

Ruler

Pencil

Acid-free spray adhesive

What You Do

1 Make a photocopy of the artwork. If you're using a black and white drawing, as in this project, you won't need to use a color photocopier. Scale it to the desired size, if necessary.

2 Color the artwork as desired. Use the felt-tipped pen to make a border around the artwork, if you want, or darken any of the lines on the copied artwork. Use the decorative-edged scissors to cut it out.

3 To mount the artwork on the foam sheet, cut out a piece of the foam that is just slightly larger than the drawing. Use the ruler as a guide when you cut the foam sheet with the craft knife, marking the lines with the pencil as necessary.

4 Follow the manufacturer's instructions and use the spray adhesive to glue the colored copy to the foam sheet. To finish, use the spray adhesive again to affix the sheet to the photo album.

Alternative: If you have a lovely drawing that is already in color, simply make a color copy and create the decorative mounting as above, in steps 3 and 4.

THOMAS TAYLOR. PENCIL AND PEN ON PAPER. 8 X 10 INCHES (20.3 x 25.4 CM). 2002.

"It is art that makes life, makes interest, makes importance, for our consideration and application of these things, and I know of no substitute whatever for the force and beauty of its process."

Henry James, writer, 1843-1916

Projects II

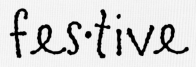

fes·tive

adj. **Befitting a festival.**

+

fab·u·lous

adj. **Astonishing.**

"Painting is silent poetry."

Plutarch, philosopher, circa 45-125

Happy Birthday Card

ARTIST:
Jaime Snyder

PROJECT DESIGNER:
Suzanne Tourtillott

Make a wish and blow out the candles! This designer took her granddaughter's original piece and transformed it into a unique expression of celebration. Preserving the original artwork by making a card allows you to share it with many others.

JAIME SNYDER. COLLAGE: FOAM SHEET ON CONSTRUCTION PAPER. 6 x 9 INCHES (15.2 x 22.9 CM). 2001.

What You Need

Blank greeting card and matching envelope

Ruler

Color photocopier

Sheet of transparent film

Craft knife

T-square

Pencil

Adhesive-backed paper, in colors that complement the artwork

Bone folder

What You Do

1 Measure the dimensions of the artwork and the greeting card, because you may need to enlarge or reduce the image so the artwork will fit on the card. For the best results, plan to keep the artwork small in relation to the card, so it will be well supported.

2 Make a color photocopy of the artwork onto the transparency material, reducing or enlarging as in step 1. Use the craft knife and ruler to trim around the transparency image, but leave a small margin of clear transparency material all the way around it.

3 Subtract the horizontal and vertical dimensions of the transparency image from those of the card. Divide these results by two for equal margins around the image, although a slightly greater bottom margin may look best, as was used in this project. Use the T-square to lightly pencil onto the front of the card where the edges and corners of the artwork will fall.

4 Cut the colored adhesive-backed paper to the same dimensions as your card. Use the T-square and the tip of the bone folder to score a center fold line onto the colored paper; score both sides well.

5 Cut the window openings in both the colored paper and in the card. You'll find it easier to position the image later if you cut the card's window just slightly larger than the artwork, but you should make the colored paper's window the same size as the artwork.

6 Remove the backing from the colored paper, but save it to use when burnishing later. Lay the colored paper with the adhesive face up and the fold line positioned horizontally before you. Adhere the transparency image over the window.

7 Keeping the card closed and the colored paper adhesive side up, position the fold of the card into the scored fold line of the colored paper. Lay down the window side of the card first, then the back. Laminate the two papers together by burnishing them with the bone folder; use the discarded backing sheet to help protect the colored paper from pressure marks.

8 Apply a few simple elements of the decorative motif to the inside of the card and to the envelope, using different colors of the adhesive-backed paper. Burnish well.

Finger Paint Gift Cards

ARTISTS:
Delaney Mai Trimble & Madison Mai Trimble

DESIGNER:
Dyan Mai Peterson

These cute gift cards are so quick and easy! It's an excellent way to proudly share the artwork of young children—these artists were only preschoolers when they created these memorable paintings.

DELANEY MAI TRIMBLE. FINGER PAINT ON PAPER.
6 x 8 INCHES (15.2 x 20.3 CM). 2000.

What You Need

Color photocopier

2 blank note cards with matching envelopes

Water-soluble felt-tip pens, in colors to match your
    artwork

2 cotton swabs

Small container of water

Paper towels

Acrylic matte medium

Foam brush

2 pieces of metallic ribbon, each 30 inches (76.2 cm)
    long

Scissors

What You Do

1 Make color copies of your artwork and scale it to size on the copier. Adjust the settings on the copier, if necessary, to assure a good color reproduction.

2 To create the torn edge on the cards, use your fingers to gently tear along the opening edge.

3 Color the torn edge of the card with a felt-tip pen. Dip a cotton swab in water, and blot off the excess water on a paper towel. Then apply the cotton swab to the inked edge of the card, which will produce a watercolor effect. Repeat for the other card, using a differently colored pen, if appropriate.

4 Apply the acrylic matte medium to the back of the color copies with the foam brush, and press into place. Allow each card to dry.

5 Cut the ribbon to the desired length, and then tie the ribbon around each card. Finish with a bow. Use a dab of glue or decoupage medium on the inside of the card to keep the ribbon in place, if desired.

"I shut my eyes in order to see."
Paul Gauguin, painter, 1848-1903

MADISON MAI TRIMBLE. FINGER PAINT AND WATERCOLOR ON PAPER. 6½ x 4½ INCHES (16.5 x 11.4 CM). 2000.

Sparkling Wire Ornament

ARTIST:
Kayla Carter

PROJECT DESIGNER:
Dietra Garden

Let the light shine through this ornament—because it's dimensional, you can enjoy it from every angle. Maybe your child has a collection of holiday art, because the only thing better than one of these ornaments is two of them.

What You Need

Photocopier

Needle-nose pliers

Wire, in various colors and gauges

Wire cutters

Beads

Clamps (optional)

Hot glue gun and glue sticks (optional)

What You Do

1 Enlarge or reduce the original artwork to approximate the size of the ornament you've planned. Using the needle-nose pliers and wire, form the outside contour of the design. Create a piece that matches the artwork in size and shape; you can use the photocopy as a pattern by setting the wire on top of the artwork and adjusting it.

2 After you've created the first contour from the wire, create a duplicate of it for this three-dimensional project. Attach the wires to each other at the top and bottom at right angles, to create four sides.

3 Once the basic form has been created and secured, use fine-gauge wire and beads to embellish the ornament and recreate the feel of the original artwork. For this Christmas tree, copper wire was used to create a garland, with glass and metal beads strung as the ornaments.

4 Use the wire of your choice to make a loop hanger for the finished ornament.

Tip: You can use clamps and hot glue to temporarily hold the basic ornament while you are creating any embellishments. An extra pair of hands might help, too!

Alternative: Make flat ornaments from any kind of artwork. Create decorations for your backyard trees from drawings of bugs and butterflies, for example.

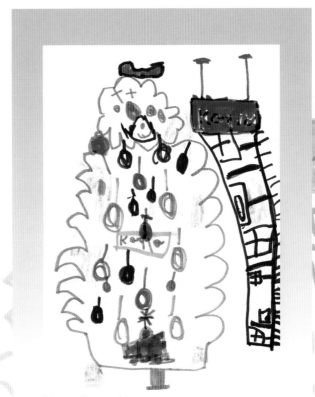

KAYLA CARTER. MARKER ON PAPER.
8 x 11 INCHES (20.3 x 27.9 CM). 2002.

Birthday Cake Platter

ARTIST:
Olivia Patterson

PROJECT DESIGNER:
Marthe Le Van

The original drawing that inspired this project was designed as a birthday greeting for the artist's younger brother. A meaningful piece of artwork like this will be everlasting if it's incorporated into a project that can be used each year on family birthdays.

OLIVIA PATTERSON. MARKER ON PAPER. 11 x 8^1/$_2$ INCHES (27.9 x 21.6). 2001.

What You Need

Scanner

Computer

Color printer

Scissors

Light-colored scrap paper

Clear glass platter, approximately 12 x 12 inches (30.5 x 30.5 cm)

Glass cleaner

Paper towels or a lint-free cloth

1-inch (2.5 cm) foam paintbrush

Matte decoupage medium

Paper punch (optional)

Assorted decorative papers (optional)

White tissue paper

2-inch (5 cm) foam paintbrush

Cutting board

Fixed-blade craft knife

Fine-tipped artist's brush

Clear spray varnish

Newspaper

Clear glass dessert plates, approximately 7¹/₂ inches (19 cm) in diameter

What You Do

1 Scan the original artwork and print it as many times as desired. Adjust the sizes of the images in your software program, if you wish. Cut out the images and position them on the platter as you go along. (This helps refine the final layout and monitor how many cutout images are ultimately needed.)

2 Place the light-colored scrap paper on your work surface, because you'll need a neutral background for the image placement. Clean the back surface of the plate with glass cleaner and a paper towel or lint-free cloth. Place the plate on the scrap paper with the back facing up.

3 Use the 1-inch (2.5 cm) paintbrush to apply an even coat of decoupage medium to the glass; make the coat of decoupage slightly larger than the surface area of the image you're decoupaging. Place the cutout in the center of the glue with the right side of the image down, facing the glue. Lightly press the paper to the surface of the glass with your fingers, forming a secure bond, and smooth out all air bubbles and wrinkles in the paper. Once you've decoupaged an image to your liking, seal it in place by applying a thin coat of glue across the back side of the image. Allow the decoupage medium to dry.

4 Repeat step 3 and adhere all remaining images. Allow the glue to dry between each paper application. If you're having trouble working in reverse, lift the plate up by its edge and turn it toward you to reconfirm image placement.

5 Here's where the fun really starts! Embellish your image any way you wish. Follow the instructions in step 3 to decoupage the decorative paper to the glass, if desired. This designer used a paper punch and origami paper to create decorative shapes and also cut three large candles out of the origami paper to place directly behind the birthday cakes. She even scanned balloon tissue paper onto the computer, reduced the size of the image, and cut them out after printing multiple copies.

6 Once the collage is complete, decoupage one large piece of white tissue paper for the background. Use the 2-inch (5 cm) paintbrush and work

quickly to apply a thin, even coating of the decoupage over the entire surface of the plate. Center the piece of tissue paper over the plate, and gently lay it down on top of the decoupage medium. Press the tissue to the glass in the middle of the plate. Use your fingers to smooth the tissue gradually across the surface of the plate. Flatten wrinkles and air pockets as you work your way to the edges. If your plate has a curved surface, some minor wrinkling will occur; fortunately, decoupaged tissue paper is so light in weight and color that the wrinkles will barely be noticeable when the glue dries. Add a second layer of tissue paper to create a deeper color by repeating this step, if desired. Allow the decoupage medium to dry longer than usual, ideally overnight.

7 Trim the excess tissue paper to a 1-inch (2.5 cm) border around the plate. With the plate upside down on the cutting board, follow around the edge of the glass with a fixed-blade craft knife and cut away all surplus tissue. Glue down any loose edges with a little decoupage medium and the fine-tipped artist's brush.

8 To use the spray varnish, work in a well-ventilated, dust-free area. Lay the decoupaged plate face-down on a surface covered with newspaper. Spray the varnish using a horizontal motion, beginning off one edge of the top of the project. Proceed with a continuous, light coat of spray across the project and off the opposite edge. Slightly overlap the layers of the varnish as you work your way down the plate. Any area of the plate missed in the initial spray will be covered in subsequent coatings. Two to three coats of varnish will adequately seal the plate.

9 Follow this same process to create dessert plates, if desired. Omit steps 6 and 7 if you choose not to have a tissue backing on the plate, although it was used in this project.

Tip: If you're new to decoupage, remember that you're working in reverse, so the images at the forefront of the design need to be applied first.

"Painting is easy when you don't know how, but very difficult when you do."

Edgar Degas, painter, 1834-1917

Trick-or-Treat Bag

ARTIST:
Devon Dickerson

PROJECT DESIGNER:
Allison Chandler Smith

Boo! This is a super-simple project that will make Halloween more memorable for your young witches, ghosts, and goblins. There'll be no quarreling over the possession of the candy from this bag, because it is personalized with the owner's artwork.

DEVON DICKERSON. INK, WATERCOLOR, AND CUT-OUT ON PAPER. 12 x 9 INCHES (30.5 x 22.9 CM). 2001.

What You Need

Photographic transfer paper

Scissors

Plain canvas bag

Iron and ironing board

What You Do

1 Take the original artwork and the photo transfer paper to a print shop. Transfer the art onto the photo transfer paper with a color photocopier. Make two copies, if you want to decorate both sides of the bag. *Note that some copy shops may not provide this service due to restrictions on the use of their copiers; call ahead to be sure that you can use this product.*

2 Cut the image out of the paper, leaving a small even border. Position the image onto the canvas bag.

3 Iron the image onto the bag according to package instructions; repeat to put an image on the other side of the bag, if desired. You might also ask your local dry cleaners to provide this service for you, since they have industrial-strength pressing equipment.

Alternative: Be earth-friendly and make up a batch of reusable grocery bags with this process; it's also a great opportunity to display lots of your children's artwork.

Digital Wrapping Paper

ARTISTS:
Dylan Shrader & Jeremy Shrader

PROJECT DESIGNER:
Valerie Shrader

These drawings of fanciful fish and graceful shells are transformed in a computer graphics program to become great wrapping paper. When you wrap a gift in this paper, the recipient gets two presents in one.

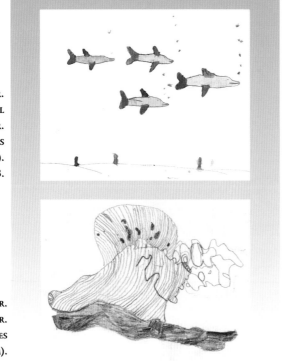

DYLAN SHRADER.
INK AND PENCIL
ON PAPER.
12 x 9 INCHES
(30.5 x 22.9 CM).
1993.

JEREMY SHRADER.
PENCIL ON PAPER.
12 x 9 INCHES
(30.5 x 22.9 CM).
1990.

What You Need

Scanner
Computer
Graphics software
Design software
Color laser printer
Color photocopier

What You Do

1 Scan the original artwork and place it into your graphics program. Adjust the image as desired, for size, color, and/or resolution. (You'll likely need lots of computer memory and available storage space for this kind of project.) Save the image after you're happy with it.

2 Import the image into a design program to create the paper. For example, two different sizes of the fish image were placed on a document that was sized for 11 x 17-inch (27.9 x 43.2 cm) paper. Copy, paste, and resize the elements as desired. Then, print onto laser paper. If you want, reduce the design and print onto 8$^{1}/_{2}$ x 11-inch (21.6 x 27.9 cm) paper to use for smaller gifts.

3 For multiple copies of your final wrapping paper, use the laser originals to make color copies on a high-quality machine. Store the wrapping paper in a flat and dry place until you need to wrap a gift, and safeguard the laser original when you need to make more paper.

Tip: This project was created at a full-service copy center, with access to a design station consisting of a computer, scanner, and color laser printer, along with the graphics and design software. If you aren't computer savvy, a full-service copy shop can scan and print for you. If you have the appropriate computer equipment and software, you can create this project easily at home, too.

Projects III

dec·o·ra·tive.

adj. Serving to adorn or embellish.

+

daz·zling

adj. To bewilder or inspire with brilliance.

"Art is not a thing; it is a way."

Elbert Hubbard, writer and philosopher, 1856-1915

Birdman Clay Tile

ARTIST:
Hannah Longley

PROJECT DESIGNER:
Dietra Garden

This drawing was part of a class project studying Navajo art and culture, and the final artwork was incorporated into a "rug" of paper. This designer captures the pictorial style of the original piece and preserves it in clay.

HANNAH LONGLEY. CRAYON AND PENCIL ON PAPER. 4 X 4 INCHES (10.2 X 10.2 CM). 2001.

What You Need

Photocopier

Low-fire red clay

Rolling pin (optional)

Fettling knife

Plastic

Slips, in colors to match the artwork

Paintbrushes

Pencil or sharp tool

Loop tool

Low-fire glazes

Kiln

What You Do

1 Reduce or enlarge the artwork to the desired size on the copier, and use this as a visual aid while you work.

2 Begin with a ¹/₂-inch (1.3 cm) slab of clay. (You can also use a rolling pin to roll the clay to the right thickness.) Cut the slab to the desired size using the fettling knife or similar tool. Lightly cover with plastic and let it dry for a day.

3 Paint the entire front of the tile with a slip (a mixture of clay and water) in the appropriate background color. It will probably need to dry for at least 24 hours.

4 Lightly draw the image onto the clay tile using the tool of your choice (anything sharp, even a pencil, will do), using the photocopy as a reference. If you need to make any corrections, rub out the design lightly with your fingertips.

5 After the design has been completed, decide which areas you want to carve. Then, use the loop tool to carve into the clay; it should have the consistency of a piece of chocolate.

6 Turn the tile over and use the fettling knife to cut out a wedge from the back to make a hanger, if you wish.

7 Now, paint the tile with slips of the desired color to match the original artwork, and then fire to cone 04. Lastly, glaze and fire to cone 06.

Alternative: Even if you're not a potter, you can make a similar project at a contemporary ceramics studio by decorating a tile that has already been fired once (bisque fired). After you have added the artwork, have the tile glaze fired at the studio.

I Love My Cat Garden Art

ARTIST AND PROJECT DESIGNER:
Terry Taylor

You'll discover how friendly this cat really is when the afternoon sun sets its eyes aglow! The designer was inspired to create this whimsical garden sculpture from his first-grade drawings saved by his mother.

TERRY TAYLOR. CRAYON ON PAPER.
14 x 8 ¹/₂ INCHES (35.6 x 21.6 CM). 1959.

What You Need

Photocopier

Scissors

18- or 20-gauge tin (from a home improvement center)

Rubber cement

Aviation or tin snips

Drill and drill bits

Jeweler's saw

File

Abrasive scrubbing pad

Hacksaw

2 feet (.6 m) of copper pipe, ¹/₂ inch (1.3 cm) in diameter

Soldering gun or propane torch

Solder

Spray enamel, in your choice of colors

Large glass jewels, in your choice of colors

Scrap of red glass

Epoxy glue

What You Do

1 Copy and enlarge your drawing. You won't need an expensive color copy for this project.

2 Cut out the copy and glue it to the tin with rubber cement.

3 Use the tin snips to cut out the image, using the copy as your guide. File the edges of the tin to remove any burrs.

4 Drill a small hole at the edge of each eye, the nose, and the mouth shapes to insert the jeweler's saw. Thread the blade in, tighten it, and cut out each feature. File the edges of each cut.

5 Peel off the paper pattern and scrub the tin with the pad to remove any glue. Using the hacksaw, make an angled cut at the end of the copper pipe. (This forms the stake so you can "plant" your garden art.) Solder the pipe to the back of the image; be sure you are working on a nonflammable surface.

6 Give the sculpture two coats of enamel paint. Allow the paint to dry between coats.

7 Glue the glass eyes, nose, and mouth to the tin with the epoxy.

Tips: Although the designer used tin to create his sculpture, it could have been made easily with plywood. When you're looking for materials, remember that stained glass shops usually have scrap boxes of glass. Ask to rummage through the box and have them cut the glass to your specifications.

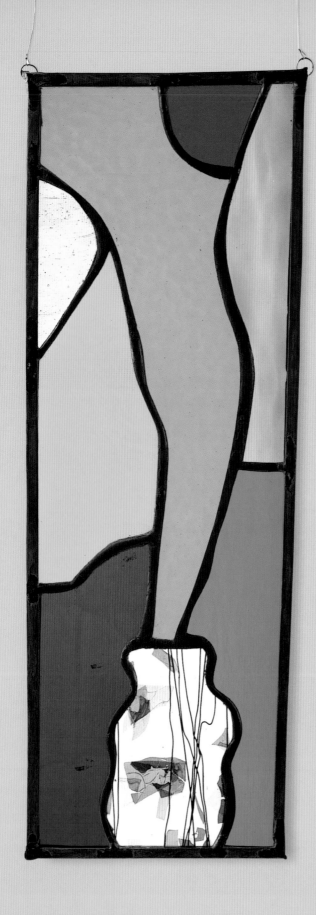

Stained Glass Panel

ARTIST:
Jaime Snyder

PROJECT DESIGNER:
Stacey Budge

Was there a genie in this bottle? It certainly seems that way. This original piece has a translucent quality, and stained glass (or its imitative technique) is the perfect medium for an interpretation of this dreamy mixed-media piece of art.

What You Need

Tracing paper

Pencil

Black felt-tipped pen

Stained glass, in the colors to match the artwork

Glass cutter

Cutting square

Pliers

Silicon carbide stone or electric glass grinder

Soap and water

1/4-inch (6 mm) black-backed copper foil

Plastic or wooden fid

Flux

Brush

60/40 solder

Soldering iron

Copper wire

Zinc strips, cut to fit the edges of the piece

Gloves

Black patina

Sponge

What You Do

1 Trace the original artwork onto the tracing paper with the pencil, changing the design to create blocks of color if necessary. Be sure to soften the acute curves and angles to make it easier to cut in glass. Use the black felt-tipped pen to go over the traced lines; this will be your working pattern.

2 Cut the straight edges of each piece first, using the cutting square. Lay the glass on top of the pattern and start at the edge of the glass, pushing the cutter along the lines of the pattern. Keep a steady pressure and continue to the end of the glass.

3 Hold the glass firmly in one hand and place the pliers next to the scored line. Grip the glass firmly with the pliers along either side of the scored line, and carefully snap the glass along the line. Cut all the shapes on the pattern.

4 Grind all the edges of each glass piece with a silicon carbide stone or an electric grinder to remove any slivers and to give the edges a matte finish to hold the copper foil.

5 Wash and dry the glass pieces and place in position on the pattern. Make any necessary adjustments to assure an exact fit.

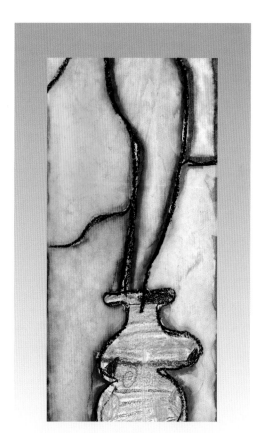

JAIME SNYDER. CRAYON AND WATERCOLOR ON PAPER. 6 X 18 INCHES (15.2 X 45.7 CM). 2001.

6 Place the edge of the piece of glass in the center of the length of foil so there is an equal amount of foil on each side of the glass edge. Wrap the foil around the edges, overlapping the ends of the foil by 1/4 inch (6 mm). Fold the edge of the foil onto the surface edges of the glass and burnish with the fid. Repeat for each piece in the design.

7 Lay the wrapped glass back in position on the pattern. Brush the foil surfaces with flux and tack the pieces together with solder. Solder the seams on both sides of the panel.

8 Fit the zinc pieces around the edges of the glass panel. Flux and solder the corners first, and then flux the rest of the zinc border and apply a thin layer of solder to all the of the zinc surfaces.

9 Cut two lengths of copper wire and then form two loops with the pliers. Solder the loops to the top corners of the panel; flux the loops and apply a thin layer of solder to the surface.

10 Wear protective gloves to apply the patina as instructed by the manufacturer. Wash the finished piece with warm soapy water and rinse in clean water.

Alternative: You don't need a soldering iron or glass grinder to create a faux stained glass piece. Look for simulated leading at your craft store, in liquid or self-adhesive forms, and buy glass paint that is translucent or transparent. Photocopy your artwork and place it under the glass, then apply the simulated leading to form the outline of your design. Paint the resulting sections as desired. Follow the manufacturer's instructions on the products for more details.

"No great artist ever sees things as they really are. If he did, he would cease to be an artist."

Oscar Wilde, writer, 1854-1900

Mermaid Frame

ARTIST:
Lucy Ballentine

PROJECT DESIGNER:
Diana Light

This busy undersea scene combines several drawings with a similar theme. If your young artist has a portfolio full of work on a related topic, consider using some of the finest in a project like this. You're sure to have plenty of vacation photos to affix to the frame.

LUCY BALLENTINE. METALLIC INK ON PAPER. 8¹/₂ x 11 INCHES (21.6 X 27.9 CM). 2002.

What You Need

Light table or sunny window

Paper

Pencil

Design template (optional)

Medium-weight aluminum, sized to fit your design

Ruler

Smooth (not corrugated) cardboard or mouse pad

Embossing tool

Spackling compound (optional)

Putty knife (optional)

One-quarter sheet of plywood, ³/₄ inch (1.9 cm) thick

Power circular saw or handsaw

Straightedge (optional)

1 yard (.9 m) of glue-backed wood edge tape

Iron

Small block of wood

Razor blade or craft knife

Fine-grit sandpaper

8 small nails

Hammer

Bolt

Cyanoacrylate glue

Toothpicks

Frame support template (page 124)

Wood glue

What You Do

1 If you don't want the artwork to be reversed on your final project, use a light table or window to trace the drawing onto another piece of paper. This is especially important if your original artwork includes numbers or letters. If you combine several drawings as this designer did, you may wish to sketch the design on another piece of paper and make a design template.

2 Tape the template (or the copy of the artwork) to the aluminum, and use the ruler to mark where it will need to be cut to the size of the template. Then, use the pencil to trace over the lines of the artwork on the template.

3 Remove the template and place the aluminum on a smooth surface, like cardboard or a mouse pad. Then, use the embossing tool or pencil to retrace the lines of the design, exerting enough pressure to emboss the metal to your satisfaction.

4 To create the space on the frame to affix the photo or artwork, turn the metal over and mark a square in the middle with the ruler and embossing

tool. Trace over it to indent the borders of the square. To insure the durability of your embossed designs, you may want to use the putty knife to fill the designs with spackling compound and let them dry before you proceed.

5 Cut the plywood to the size of your template, using a handsaw or power circular saw. (If you use a power saw, clamp on a straightedge to use as a guide for the saw.) Now, cut the aluminum to the final size of your frame, plus an additional $1/16$ inch (1.6 mm) all around. The frame shown here is $8^1/_2$ x $8^1/_2$ inches (21.6 x 21.6 cm).

6 Cover the exposed edges of the plywood with the wood tape. Use an iron at its hottest setting to press over the wood tape to warm the glue, and then press firmly on it with a block of wood. Make sure the surfaces make a strong bond.

7 Use a razor blade or craft knife to trim away the excess tape and sand the edges until smooth.

8 Hammer the aluminum to the frame, placing a bolt between the hammer and the nail to avoid marring the aluminum. Place four of the nails around the inside corners of the photo square, and place the other four on the outside corners of the frame itself. Gently hammer the edges of the aluminum around the edges of the frame to bend it over the sides.

9 If necessary, use a toothpick to apply cyanoacrylate glue to any gaps in the frame.

10 Use the template on page 124 to create the frame support. Cut this piece from the plywood, making sure one side is 7 to 10° off vertical per the template. Affix it to the frame with wood glue.

Alternative: No woodworking skills? Not to worry—you can also create this project using a store-bought frame as a base.

Starry Night Linens

ARTIST:
Olivia Patterson

PROJECT DESIGNER:
Diana Light

This project is a great example of using a simple yet lovely piece of artwork to beautifully adorn your home. Delightful designs like this are easy to embroider; try this technique on table linens, too. Look carefully to find the surprise under the sheets.

What You Need

Set of sheets with matching pillowcase

Photocopier

Craft knife or scissors

Fabric marking pencil

Embroidery needle

Embroidery floss, in colors to match the artwork

Fabric scissors or snips

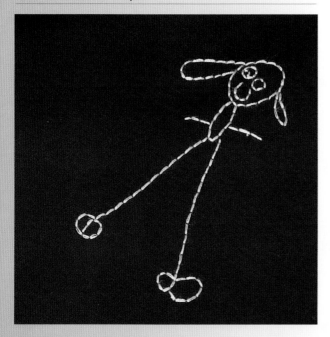

What You Do

1 If you are using 100 percent cotton linens, wash them first to allow for shrinkage.

2 Make a photocopy of the original artwork. To transfer the design, make stencils from the artwork by cutting out the designs. Then, place the design onto the linens at the desired location and trace around them with the marking pencil. (The designs in this project are placed in the center of the sheet.) If you prefer, you can duplicate the designs freehand with the marking pencil, or transfer them with dressmaker's tracing paper.

3 Use a single strand of floss to embroider the design; the simple satin stitch is perfect to create this particular project. Use more elaborate stitches if it's in keeping with the spirit of your original artwork.

OLIVIA PATTERSON. MARKER AND PENCIL ON PAPER. 8½ x 11 INCHES (21.6 x 27.9 CM). 2000.

Mother Earth Silk Pillow

ARTIST:
Erika Swiger

PROJECT DESIGNER:
Radian Nesbitt

This pillow is a cheerful rendering of how one child views the world—and what a peaceful and friendly place it is. The silk-resist dying process complements the original watercolor painting, and the designer added just a bit of color to accent the peoples of the earth.

What You Need

Iron and ironing board

Freezer paper

2 white silk scarves, each 11 x 11 inches (27.9 x 27.9 cm)

Copy of original artwork (optional)

Pencil

Silk dyeing kit

Small watercolor brush (size 4 or 6)

Small plastic watercolor palette

Towel

Sewing machine

Thread, to match the fabric color

Polyester fiberfill

What You Do

1 Iron the freezer paper to the silk pieces, waxed side facing the silk. Place the child's drawing (or a photocopy) underneath the silk. Trace the design on the pillow with a pencil. (You'll leave the freezer paper on the silk until it is completely dyed and dry.)

2 Using the resist from the silk dyeing kit, trace the pencil lines. Allow the resist to dry; it will prevent the dyes from bleeding into one another when they are painted on the silk.

3 When the resist is dry, apply the dyes with a small watercolor brush. Be sure to rinse your brush in water after using each color. A small plastic watercolor palette is great for this step, since you can mix or combine the colors to get the shade you want.

4 After the painting is complete, let it dry completely. Remove the freezer paper from the silk by gently pulling it away from the fabric. Follow the

directions in the kit for setting the dyes. After rinsing out the solution, wrap the wet silk in a towel to remove some of the dampness, and then press the silk with the iron set on the lowest setting.

5 To make the pillow, put the silk pieces right sides together and stitch around the edges, leaving an opening to stuff the pillow. Turn right side out and fill the pillow with the fiberfill. Slipstitch the opening.

Alternative: Instead of using silk for both sides of the pillow, use brightly colored cotton for the back. Choose a color that matches the original artwork.

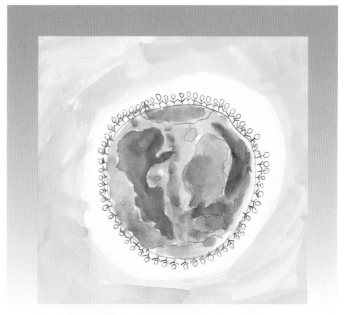

ERIKA SWIGER. PENCIL AND WATERCOLOR ON PAPER. 14 X 11 INCHES (35.6 X 27.9 CM). 2001.

Leaf Print Table Runner

ARTIST:
Katrina O'Shields

PROJECT DESIGNER:
Dietra Garden

For this contemporary table runner, the original piece of artwork was used to stamp the decorative squares. You could easily create matching napkins with this technique, too. The soothing tones of this piece are the perfect backdrop for a casual dinner with friends or family.

What You Need

Tape measure

2 yards (1.8 m) of cotton canvas

Scissors

Ruler

Cardboard template (optional)

Fabric dye, in the color of your choice

Washing machine

Salt (optional)

Clothes dryer

Iron and ironing board

Natural, unbleached muslin

Carved rubber or linoleum block

Oil-based inks, in the colors of your choice

Ink tray

Brayer (optional)

Pencil

Sewing machine

Silver metallic thread

What You Do

1 Measure your table and cut the canvas to the desired length; the width should be about 12 inches (30.5 cm). Use a ruler to mark off the triangular ends, or cut out a cardboard template to trace; then, trim the ends.

2 Dye the fabric in your washing machine according to the dye manufacturer's instructions. Rinse with salt to help retain the color. Dry the fabric completely and iron as needed; the luxurious fringe on this table runner is created during the washing and drying process, with no effort on your part!

3 Cut some patches from the muslin that approximate the size of the original block carving. Then, print the image onto the muslin squares; use the brayer to apply the ink, if necessary. Be sure to use an oil-based ink, so the table runner can be laundered.

4 After the patches have dried, arrange them on the cloth to your liking. Then, trace around the corners with a pencil to mark their placement. (You could also pin them on, if desired.) Make a sketch and number the patches, if necessary. Then, sew the patches onto the table runner at the appropriate spots, using silver metallic thread and a small zigzag stitch.

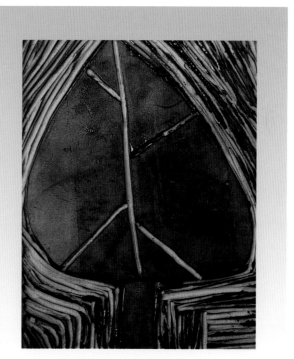

KATRINA O'SHIELDS. CARVED RUBBER BLOCK.
3 x 4 INCHES (7.6 x 10.2 CM). 2001.

Abstract Paintings

ARTIST:
Triston Jaynes

DESIGNER:
Valerie Shrader

These paintings look like they belong in a gallery, since they have been transferred to canvas and treated just like pieces of fine art. Though the images aren't a matched pair, each has its own character and complements the other.

What You Need

1 yard (.9 m) of canvas

Scissors

Stretchers, sized for your artwork

Staple gun and staples

Frames (if desired)

What You Do

1 Take the original artwork and the canvas to your digital imaging shop. Have the personnel at the shop prepare the fabric transfer and place it on the canvas according to your size specifications; these pieces were enlarged to be close to 11 x 17 inches (17.9 x 43.2 cm).

2 Cut the two pieces out of the canvas. Assemble the stretchers and place the pieces on the stretchers, stapling them to the back of the stretchers as you go. If you want to frame them, do it yourself or take them to a professional to be framed.

Tip: Look for tightly woven yet somewhat flexible canvas for this project; actual artist's canvas may not be forgiving enough for this process. Before you buy any fabric, check with your local imaging professionals for their recommendations, because a thin fabric may not withstand the heat transfer process, while one that is too thick may not give you a satisfactory reproduction.

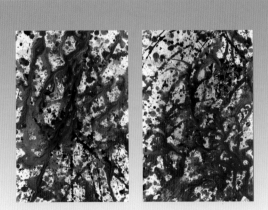

TRISTON JAYNES. FINGER PAINT ON PAPER.
5 x 8 INCHES (12.7 x 20.3 CM). 2001.

That Girl! Fabric Doll

ARTIST:
Corrina Matthews

PROJECT DESIGNER:
Terry Taylor

What better way to preserve a child's view of the fashion of the moment? If they've forgotten jewelry, and perhaps the colors, too, apply your own imagination to the world of kid couture. This technique will work for cuddly creatures, too.

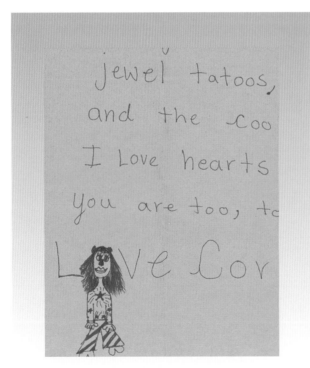

CORINNA MATTHEWS. INK ON CONSTRUCTION PAPER. 9 X 12 INCHES (22.9 X 30.5 CM). 2001.

What You Need

Photocopier

Tape

1/2 yard (45.7 cm) of white cotton fabric

Pencil

Newspaper or cardboard

Waxed paper

Fabric paints and markers

Pins and pincushion

Needle

White thread

Sewing machine (optional)

Polyester fiberfill

Measuring tape

Yarn, in the color of your choice

Carpet thread, to match the yarn

Beads (optional)

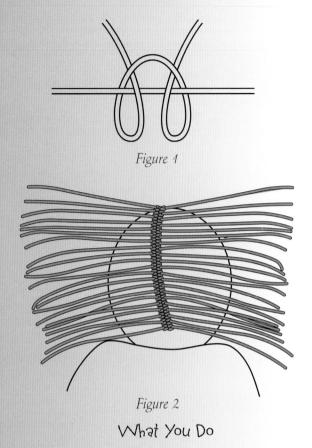

Figure 1

Figure 2

What You Do

1 Photocopy your drawing and enlarge, if necessary.

2 Tape the photocopy to a window (or a light box, if you have one). Tape the fabric over the photocopy. Trace the drawing lightly with the pencil. Trace any details of the drawing, too, like stripes, facial features, and so forth. Remove the fabric from the light source.

3 Repeat the process in step 2, this time turning over the image to be traced. Trace the reverse of the image, including the details as in step 2. Now you have two mirror images on the same piece of fabric, one for the front of the doll and the other for the back.

4 Place a sheet of waxed paper on the newspaper or cardboard, and place the fabric flat on top of the waxed paper.

5 Paint both sides of the figure as desired. Let them dry thoroughly before you cut them out.

6 Put the two figures together, with the right (painted) sides facing. Pin them together. Cut out around the figures leaving a 1/2-inch (1/3 cm) seam allowance.

7 With the right sides still together, stitch the seam by hand or by machine. Leave a section open to insert the stuffing. Clip any curves as needed, and turn the figure right side out.

8 Stuff the figure as desired. Stitch the opening closed by hand.

9 To make the hair, measure the doll's head from the forehead to the nape of the neck. Measure and cut out a piece of cardboard 6 inches (15.2 cm) long and as wide as the measurement of the doll's head. Make two small notches on either side of the width of the cardboard.

10 Tie a length of carpet thread around the width of the cardboard, allowing the thread to rest in the notches. Cut 12-inch (30.5 cm) lengths of yarn and set them aside.

11 Double a length of yarn. Slip the loop under the carpet thread and bring the ends through the loop, as in figure 1. Cover the thread with knotted yarn, using both sides of the cardboard.

12 Slip the hair from the cardboard and tie the ends of the carpet thread. Double it over and pin it in place on the back of the head with the knotted edges forming a part, as in figure 2. Sew the hair to the head with an overcast stitch, catching both sides of the part. Trim the hair to the desired length.

13 Stitch some beads to the figure to create jewelry, if desired. This doll has necklace of beads, too.

Folk Art Magnetic Board

ARTIST:
Daniel Henderson

PROJECT DESIGNER:
Dietra Garden

There's something slightly amazing about this project: all the elements can be rearranged to create a new piece of art. This is an interactive project that the whole family can enjoy—the more elements in your drawing, the more fun it will be.

DANIEL HENDERSON. CRAYON AND PENCIL ON PAPER. 12 x 18 INCHES (30.5 x 45.7 CM). 2001.

What You Need

Steel sheet, $\frac{1}{8}$-inch (3 mm) thick

Circular saw with metal cutting blade

Small motorized rotary tool

Rust inhibitor spray

Color photocopier

Scissors

Pencil

Adhesive magnetic sheets, enough for your artwork

Craft wire

Felt dots (optional)

What You Do

1 Cut the steel sheet to the desired size with a metal cutting saw blade. (This project is 11 x 17 inches [27.9 x 43.2 cm].) Smooth the edges of the metal with the rotary tool, then use it to drill two holes in the top of the steel for the wire hanger.

2 If desired, sand, scratch, or otherwise apply any textural designs to the steel board. Then, treat with rust inhibitor spray.

3 Make color photocopies of the art and reduce or enlarge as desired. Have the copies laminated and cut out the individual images. Then, trace these images onto the magnetic sheet and cut them out just a little bit smaller than the original pieces so the magnetic paper doesn't show.

4 Peel the protective paper from the magnetic sheet and place the images onto it. Put the magnetized images on the steel sheet to replicate the original drawing, or move them around to create a new picture.

5 Insert the wire through the holes and twist the ends around the wire to secure them. To avoid scratching the wall where you install the steel hanging, attach felt dots to each corner on the back of the metal, if desired.

Alternative: For a little literary fun, make some magnetized words and letters to accompany your artwork.

Day of the Dead Sconce

ARTIST:
Devon Dickerson

PROJECT DESIGNER:
Dana Irwin

Take a vibrant piece of artwork, like this piece done to commemorate Dia de los Muertos, and use simple tools and materials to make a stunning mask sconce. A similar piece of ethnic art would make an equally impressive piece when you punch out the outlines of the drawing.

What You Need

Aluminum roofing tin

Fine-tipped black marker

Tin snips or scissors

Stack of newspapers

Hammer

Nails of different sizes

Chisel

Cloth

Rubbing Alcohol

Acrylic paint, in colors to match your artwork

Paintbrush

Metal scouring pad

Craft wire

Clear acrylic sealer spray

What You Do

1 Trace the design onto the roofing tin with the marker. Use the tin snips to cut out the sconce from the tin.

2 Put a 1-inch (2.5 cm) stack of newspapers underneath the metal. Using the hammer, nails, and/or chisel, punch holes into the sconce where desired.

3 To prepare the surface for painting, use a cloth and alcohol to remove any oil from the sconce. Then, paint with acrylic paint as desired.

4 Let the sconce dry completely. Distress the aluminum by rubbing with the scouring pad, allowing the base metal to shine through the sconce as desired.

5 Punch holes on either side of the sconce and insert the craft wire; this will hold the sconce over your light fixture.

6 Spray on the clear acrylic to seal the surface.

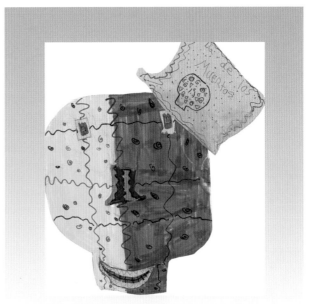

DEVON DICKERSON. MARKER ON HEAVY PAPER;
CONSTRUCTION PAPER HAT.
9 x 14 INCHES (22.9 x 35.6 CM). 2001.

Geometric Window Shade

ARTIST:
Dylan Shrader

DESIGNER:
Valerie Shrader

Take a child's simple design and use it as a decorating motif. Here, this study of geometric shapes is the basis for a sponge-painted window shade. Try this on linens or a lampshade, too, or even as a border along your walls.

What You Need

Window shade

Ruler

Pencil

Compressed sponges

Acrylic paints, in colors to match your artwork

Plate or bowl

What You Do

1 To reproduce this type of design, divide the shade into squares for painting. First, decide how large you want the design, and then measure the shade. Divide the shade by the number of squares you want, and make faint guide marks on the shade with the pencil to indicate the sections that will be painted different colors. Mark areas on both the top and bottom of the shade on which to paint the design.

2 Cut the sponges into pieces that correspond to the sizes of the designs within the squares. Cut an additional rectangular piece to use while painting the background coat; for this project, the rectangular piece was a quarter the size of the square itself. Wet the compressed sponges to hydrate them.

3 Paint the background coat first, dipping the sponge into a plate or bowl of paint and letting it absorb the color. Sponge onto the border as desired, using both vertical and horizontal applications of the sponge for visual interest. Let the background dry before proceeding to the next step.

4 Prepare to paint the geometric designs themselves by hydrating the sponge shapes. Then, choose one of the colors and apply it to the background, beginning at the edge of the square. Let the first color dry thoroughly.

5 Sponge on the remaining color. Let the shade dry completely before you install it.

Tip: Geometric designs like these are easy to duplicate using simple tools and procedures (and a little simple math, too). If you have experience with stamp carving or stenciling, you could easily use these methods to decorate a shade using a design based on a more complex piece of artwork.

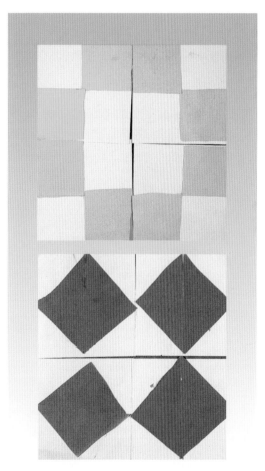

DYLAN SHRADER. CONSTRUCTION PAPER COLLAGE. 8 x 8 INCHES (20.3 x 20.3 CM). 1993.

Three Generations Gourd

ARTISTS:
Delaney Mai Trimble, Madison Mai Trimble, & Ember Mai Trimble

DESIGNER AND ARTIST:
Dyan Mai Peterson

This easy-to-make family heirloom gourd can be passed down for generations to come, because gourds will last for thousands of years if they are kept dry and out of the sun. The crayon decoration is actually quite simple, so this is a good project for the whole family.

DELANEY MAI TRIMBLE. PENCIL AND MARKER ON PAPER.
11 x 8¹/₂ INCHES (27.9 x 21.6 CM). 2000.

What You Need

Tall kettle gourd, cleaned

Water

Scrub brush

Pencil

Hacksaw

Dust mask

Block of wood

Scraping tool or grapefruit spoon

Black flat enamel spray paint

Leather dyes, in the colors of your choice

2 foam brushes, each 1 inch (2.5 cm) wide

Paper towels

Cotton swabs

Photocopier

Tape

Transfer paper

Box of 24 color crayons

Hair dryer

Color felt-tipped pens (optional)

Clear satin lacquer spray

Awl

6 inches (15.2 cm) of waxed linen thread

Beads

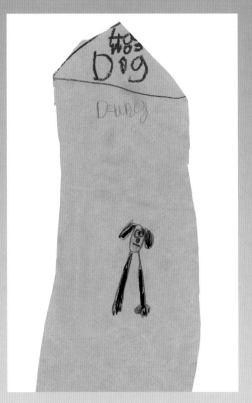

DELANEY MAI TRIMBLE. CRAYON AND COLORED PENCIL ON CONSTRUCTION PAPER. 4 x 10 INCHES (10.2 x 25.4 CM). 2000.

DELANEY MAI TRIMBLE. MARKER ON PAPER. 8$^{1}/_{2}$ x 11 INCHES (21.6 x 27.9 CM). 2002.

EMBER MAI TRIMBLE. PENCIL ON PAPER. 4$^{1}/_{2}$ x 7 INCHES (11.4 x 17.8 CM). 1977.

What You Do

1 Clean the outside of the gourd with warm water and a scrub brush; remove the dirt and mold, but be careful not to scratch the surface. Allow to dry.

2 Use a pencil to draw a cut line all around the top of the gourd. Make a few short strokes with the saw to start cutting along the line. (Remember to wear a dust mask!) Cut evenly straight through the neck of the gourd, holding the gourd firmly with your free hand. To help support the gourd while you are cutting, rest the neck on a block of wood.

3 After you've cut the opening of the gourd, clean the inside with a scraping tool to remove the pulp and seeds, continuing to wear the dust mask. Spray the inside of the gourd with black enamel spray paint and let it dry.

4 Next, dye the outside of the gourd. To create the effect used on this gourd, coat the entire surface with buckskin leather dye, using the foam brush. While the dye is still moist, apply brown dye to the top 2 inches (5.1 cm) of the gourd. The shading effect is achieved by blending the brown dye down and into the buckskin dye with a paper towel.

5 Dip a cotton swab into black leather dye, if desired, and apply it around the top 1/2 inch (1.3 cm) of the gourd rim. You can hasten the drying time with a hair dryer, if desired.

6 Reduce or enlarge the artwork you want to place on the gourd; the size of the patterns should be in proportion to the gourd. Tape the transfer paper and the artwork copies to the gourd and trace over the design with a pencil.

7 Now, trace over the transferred designs with the crayons, using the desired colors; you may need to trace over them several times. (Felt-tipped pens are another option for this step, too.) Set the hair dryer to a low temperature and slowly melt the crayon tracings, using just enough heat to melt them—if the crayon gets too hot, it will drip down the gourd.

8 To seal the gourd and protect your design, apply a fine mist of lacquer and allow it to dry. Apply a second coat and let dry. Be careful not to use too much spray in any one coat, or it may run and create drips.

9 Use the awl to poke two holes next to one another, about 1 inch (2.5 cm) down from the rim of the gourd. Insert the waxed linen thread through the holes and tie a knot on the outside of the gourd. Add beads to the thread, and then tie a knot at the end of the thread to hold the beads in place.

Tip: If you have some empty spaces between the pieces of artwork, you can add circles, swirls, dots, etc., as design elements.

MADISON MAI TRIMBLE. MARKER ON PAPER, MOUNTED ON CONSTRUCTION PAPER. 17 X 11 INCHES (43.2 X 27.9 CM). 2001.

Picnic Tablecloth

ARTIST:
Karlie Budge

PROJECT DESIGNER:
Stacey Budge

Pack up the picnic basket with your favorite foods and spend an afternoon lounging on this homespun tablecloth. A little sewing experience is all that's needed to make this project, and most any type of drawing can be repeated in the border.

KARLIE BUDGE. MARKER ON PAPER. 11 x 8¹/₂ INCHES (27.9 x 21.6 CM). 2002.

What You Need

1/2 yard (45.7 cm) of white cotton muslin

Tape measure

Scissors

Scanner

Computer

Graphics software program

Inkjet printer

Inkjet fabric transfer paper

Pins and pincushion

Iron and ironing board

Sewing machine

Thread, to match the fabric color

1 1/4 yards (1.1 cm) of contrasting decorative cotton
fabric, the same weight as the muslin

Fabric marking pencil

What You Do

1 Cut four strips of muslin, each 4 x 31 1/2 inches (10.2 x 80 cm), and cut four squares of muslin, each 4 x 4 inches (10.2 x 10.2 cm).

2 Scan in the original artwork, and scale it in your graphics program to be no larger that 3 1/2 inches (8.9 cm) high. Print out enough copies on the inkjet transfer paper to fill your white muslin strips and corner pieces.

3 Apply the transfers onto the muslin strips and corner pieces as directed by the manufacturer. Be sure to leave a 1/4-inch (6 mm) seam allowance at all edges.

4 With the right sides together, pin a muslin square to the left edge of a muslin strip. Stitch along the edge using a 1/4-inch (6 mm) seam allowance. Repeat with the other three strips and squares of muslin.

5 Cut a 31 1/2 x 31 1/2-inch (80 x 80 cm) square out of the contrasting fabric (See figure 1 for the arrangement of the strips and contrasting fabric.) With right sides together, pin one muslin strip to the edge of the fabric square, placing the seam in the muslin strip 1/4 inch (6 mm) in from the edge of the fabric square, aligned with the seam allowance at the left. Begin stitching the seam here, using a 1/4-inch (6 mm) seam allowance. (See figure 2—you will need this seam allowance to finish the border.)

6 Place the next strip at the right edge of the contrasting fabric, right sides together, and pin. Stitch the seam. Repeat to sew the remaining muslin strips to the fabric square to form a border. When you stitch the final side, stop when you meet the initial seam. Pin the unfinished edge of the muslin strip to the muslin square, clipping it if necessary, and stitch. Clip the other corners as needed and press the seams open.

7 Cut four 4 x 40-inch (10.2 x 101.6 cm) strips out of contrasting fabric. Fold one of the contrasting fabric strips in half lengthwise and iron flat. Fold the edges in, meeting at the center, and press again. Repeat for all four contrasting fabric strips.

8 Measure and mark the white muslin border 1/4 inch (6 mm) from the edge. Pin the folded strips around the raw edge of the tablecloth, aligning it with the marked line. The edging will extend 1 inch (2.5 cm) on either side of the tablecloth. Sew the edging to the tablecloth very close to the fold, leaving 1 1/2 inches (3.8 cm) at the corners open. Repeat for the other edges.

9 To finish the corners, overlap the left edge over the right edge, fold the raw edges under at an angle to give it a mitered edge, and pin. Stitch. Repeat with the other corners and press flat.

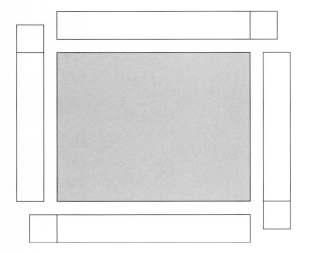

Figure 1

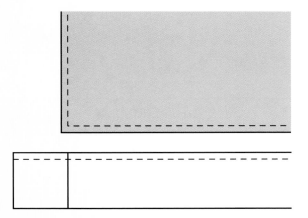

Figure 2

KARLIE BUDGE. MARKER ON PAPER. 11 X 8½ INCHES (27.9 X 21.6 CM). 2002.

Extended Frame Painting

ARTIST:
Jessica Van Arsdale

PROJECT DESIGNER:
Dana Irwin

Here's a project that makes wonderful use of the original piece of artwork. If you and your child both paint, here's an excellent way to combine your talents. Use the motifs from your child's painting and continue them onto the frame that you decorate.

What You Need

Flat wooden frame, to fit your artwork

Sandpaper

White latex paint, plus colors to match the original artwork

Paintbrushes

Color photocopy of the original artwork

Pencil (optional)

Sheet of clear acrylic or glass (optional)

What You Do

1 Remove the glass and sand the surface of the frame; clean any dust from the surface.

2 Paint the entire frame white.

3 Photocopy the art and place it into the frame for reference. Expand on the original artwork by extending the design onto the frame, creating elements on the front, inner, and outer edges of the frame, too. Begin by painting the background color, then adding any decorative elements. Sketch a basic design on the frame with a pencil, if necessary, but try to use the same painting techniques as the artist.

4 Paint the extended design, matching the colors of the original artwork. Add any flourishes as desired, like the dots of color in this project.

5 Place the original painting back into the frame when it's completely dry. Use a sheet of clear acrylic or glass to protect original painting, if desired.

JESSICA VAN ARSDALE. OIL ON CANVAS. 8 x 10 INCHES (20.3 x 25.4 CM). 2001.

Enchanted Wainscoting

ARTIST:
Anna Wells

PROJECT DESIGNER:
Diana Light

Were these merry frogs once princes? Anything is possible when fairies and magic are involved. You'll be surprised at how easy it is to transfer a group of whimsical sketches into this divine decorating project. If your child likes to doodle or cartoon, you'll have plenty of great original art.

What You Need

Photocopier

Ruler or straightedge

Pencil

Painter's tape

Transfer paper

Paintbrushes, including a 1-inch (2.5 cm), 2-inch
(5 cm), and detail brush

6 colors of latex paint

Black acrylic craft paint

Lumber, in the desired height and
width (optional)

Paint, to match the existing wall (optional)

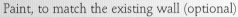
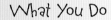

What You Do

1 Plan the size of your wainscoting, and then photocopy the various designs that you plan to incorporate. Scale them to the proper size, if necessary.
(You don't need a color photocopier for this project.)

2 Determine the height of your wainscoting.
Measure and mark the placement of the horizontal row at the top with a series of pencil dots, and
place a length of tape all along the wall at your chosen height. Make sure to apply the tape in a straight
line along the wall. Then, measure, mark, and tape the
bottom of the horizontal row. Add a line of tape to
divide this horizontal row into two, as in this project,
if desired. Measure, mark, and tape every other vertical row of your design.

3 Paint the top horizontal row in the color of your
choice. Remove the tape as soon as you have
painted the row. Let this section dry, then add a new
line of tape to use as a guide for the second horizontal
row. Paint in your chosen color.

4 To add geometric designs, like the triangles used
in this project, use tape to mark the areas and
then paint. Let these designs dry before you proceed.

5 Now, paint the first set of vertical stripes in your
chosen colors; remove the tape immediately.
When these alternating rows are dry, add a new line
of tape to delineate the remaining rows and paint
those. Let the rows dry.

6 Here comes the fun part! Now, use the transfer
paper and pencil to mark your chosen designs
onto the appropriate vertical row. Paint over the transferred designs with the detail brush and black acrylic
paint. Let the wall dry thoroughly before you place
any furniture nearby.

7 If desired, add a piece of lumber as a finishing
touch. Here, it's painted the same color as the
existing wall.

**ANNA WELLS. PEN AND MARKER ON PAPER. 11 x 8½ INCHES (27.9
x 21.6 CM). 2001.**

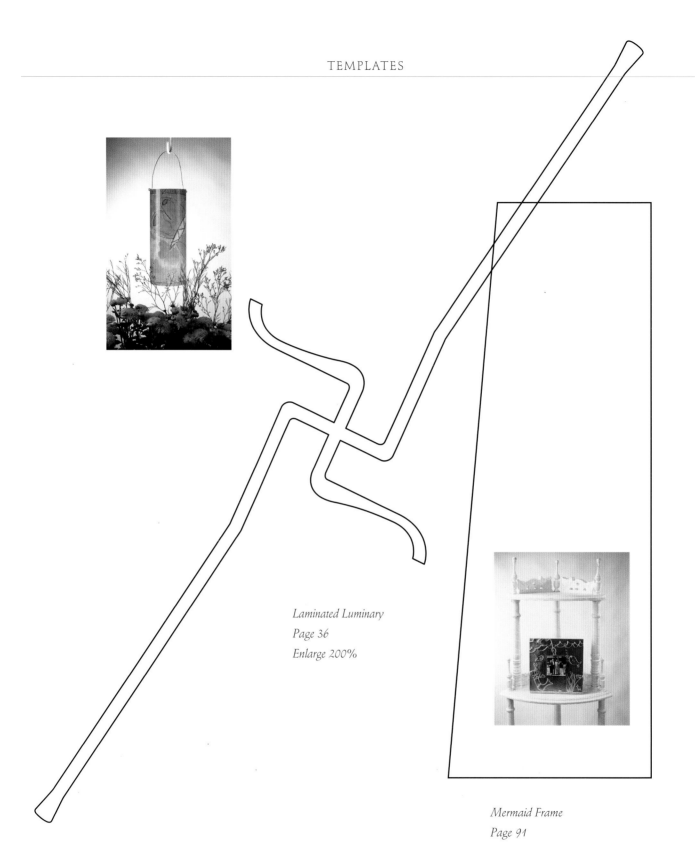

Laminated Luminary
Page 36
Enlarge 200%

Mermaid Frame
Page 91

STACEY BUDGE is an art director at Lark Books. When she is not using her creative talents to design books, she can be found crafting and gardening at her home in Asheville, North Carolina.

DIETRA GARDEN, an art educator and free-lance designer, is constantly tinkering with new materials and techniques for artistic expression and creative utility to the benefit (and occasional amusement) of her husband Sean and family of animals: Jake, Ruby, and Junior.

DANA IRWIN. See Artist Profiles.

CORINNE KURZMANN leads an eclectic life in Asheville, North Carolina, with her husband Bob, 10 children, two hounds, one cat, and a large garden. She owns Diggin Art, a landscape company, and is a frequent contributor to Lark publications.

MARTHE LE VAN first encountered a decoupaged glass plate while rummaging at a local antique shop. Inspired to make her own, she has been cheerfully decoupaging glassware ever since. Marthe has created projects for several Lark publications, including *The Decorated Frame, Nature Style, Simple Glass Crafts,* and *Creative Tabletop Fountains,* all published in 2002.

DIANA LIGHT is an accomplished artisan who specializes in functional art—turning any object into something beautiful and useful. She is the author of *The Weekend Crafter: Etching Glass* (Lark Books, 2000), and has designed projects for many Lark books. Contact her at dianalight@hotmail.com.

RADIAN NESBITT has spent many years teaching art to children of all ages, but her favorite teaching methods allow the child to create something useful and fun at the same time. She is a silk painter and a watercolorist, and travels to festivals, shows, galleries, and shops to display her work. She also designs her own silk cloth.

PAMELA PADDOCK loves working with wood, creating fun, functional art like clocks, mirrors, and lamps. She has a Bachelor of Fine Arts from Florida Atlantic University.

DYAN MAI PETERSON is an internationally known gourd artist and teacher. She is the author of *The Decorated Gourd* (Lark Books, 2002), and her work is featured in several galleries. She is a member of he Southern Highlands Craft Guild, and lives in the beautiful mountains of Western North Carolina.

JEANNE PULLEYN is an avid knitter and knitting designer. Besides her role as grandmother, Jeanne is, at 79 years old, involved in regional planning and local government in North Haven, Connecticut, and racks up championship scores at bowling. She has knit over 500 garments in her life.

ALLISON CHANDLER SMITH has a home-based business specializing in providing deluxe tourist accommodations in remote locations in Western North Carolina. She is also an avid crafter and designer in addition to being a full-time mother. She has created projects for numerous Lark books, including *Decorating Baskets* (2002), *Girls' World* (2002), and *Decorating Candles* (2001). She lives in Asheville, North Carolina.

TERRY TAYLOR. See Artist Profiles.

SUZANNE TOURTILLOTT lives the good life in Asheville, North Carolina. She enjoys using transfer methods of all kinds, and makes her living multitasking like crazy.

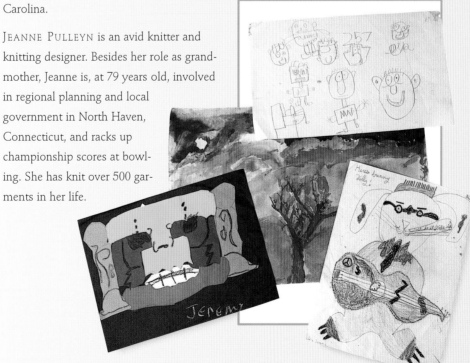

DJANGO BALLENTINE has been drawing since he could hold a pencil, and published his first poem at age two. He is home schooled, which allows him to read until 11 P.M. Django also studies Spanish and Japanese, and recently began performing on stage, appearing as Benjamin in *Joseph and the Amazing Technicolor Dream Coat.*

LUCY BALLENTINE is almost seven years old, adores swimming, and studies modern dance. She is wild about riding horses and is looking forward to summer camp. Lucy is home schooled.

KARLIE BUDGE loves to draw animals. But  she also loves to dance, so she may star as a Radio City Rockette before she goes to veterinary school. Karlie has a while to decide on a career, since she is just seven years old.

KAYLA CARTER is a kindergarten student and loves riding her bike. When she hops off, she also likes to play with her dolls. She wants to be a ballerina and a college teacher when she outgrows her dolls. Kayla's five now.

DEVON DICKERSON created some of the artwork featured in this book when she was in the third grade. Now 10 years old, Devon enjoys skateboarding, playing softball, basketball, reading, and wrestling with her little sister.

THOMAS GOODWIN says he is going to be a crocodile hunter when he grows up! He's five years old and loves animals.

QUILLAN HUNT is a soccer player and is now in the seventh grade. He also likes to draw and create his own cards when he takes off his soccer cleats.

DANIEL HENDERSON says "Hi!" He likes  all sports, but especially enjoys skateboarding. Daniel is 11 years old and has fun drawing, too.

BRIANNA HUSKEY has been pursuing artistic endeavors since she was four years old; she's now 12. Her interests include writing poetry and drawing, but she also works in a wide range of mixed media.

DANA IRWIN is an artist who enjoys an active life with her three dogs and two cats in Asheville, North Carolina. She has been a teacher of art at elementary, high school and college levels. She is an art director at Lark Books and has created many projects for many Lark books over many years.

TRISTON JAYNES, age seven, likes baseball and art. He has a great imagination and creates some really neat stuff.

MILES KURZMANN is into computers and math. Even though he is only 11 and in mid-  dle school, he has already picked out his college—Duke University in Durham, North Carolina.

HANNAH LONGLEY enjoys drawing, writing, and being with her family. She is crazy about animals and would like to be a veterinarian and an artist. Hannah is seven.

OLIVIA MADDIX, who's four, stays busy trying to keep up with her nine-year-old brother. She loves her cat, Sophie, and likes to garden with her mother. Her mother says she is bossy and thus will be a great business executive one day!

CORINNA MATTHEWS is 11 years old and  has been exploring a variety of art media for years. She is a natural-born stylist and interior decorator, too; she proves it by rearranging her bedroom every few months! One of her favorite "canvases" for artistic expression is a plain cardboard box, because the possibilities are endless.

KATRINA O'SHIELDS loves drawing and art. If she doesn't become a professional soccer player, she'll consider being an art teacher. She is eight years old.

OLIVIA PATTERSON is now seven years old. She likes nature, art, stories, and especially her brother, Joseph—one of her pieces featured in this book was created for him.

MICAH PULLEYN has an undergraduate degree in art history and she did graduate work at the University of Iowa at the Center for the Book. She is an avid papermaker and bookmaker, and has taught both crafts at several colleges. In addition, she teaches art to kids, and is deep in the turmoil of fixing up an old house. She still draws pretty pictures but has never learned to knit. She lives in Asheville, North Carolina.

DYLAN SHRADER is a teenage guitar player  now, but he used to really love trains. He also runs cross country and writes for his high school newspaper. If the music thing doesn't work out, he might study marine biology. Dylan wants a sports car, but he probably won't get one.

JEREMY SHRADER, a college senior, plans to stay in school until he  can figure out what he wants to do when he grows up! Actually, he's busy pursuing a double major and is interested in marketing. Jeremy is a writer and photographer, and is one of the captains of the university soccer team.

JAIME SNYDER loves math, reading, and taking field trips at school—but she also digs swimming, dance lessons, and making crafts. She hopes to be an archeologist some day.

ERIKA SWIGER was inspired to create the watercolor featured in this book while vacationing at the beach. She is very con-  cerned about the environment and wants to make the world a better place to live. Erika loves all animals and wants to be a marine biologist. She's now 10 years old.

TERRY TAYLOR is a mixed media artist whose work has been shown in numerous exhibitions. He is the  full-time craft guru at Lark Books.

THOMAS TAYLOR is a student at Enka Middle School in Candler, North Carolina and an avid snow skier. He dreams of becoming a Blue Devil at Duke University, which should help in his desire to become a medical researcher.

DELANEY MAI TRIMBLE is eight years old and likes to make every-  one happy. She's wild about soccer and riding horses, and she's also an avid reader. Her artwork has won several contests. Delaney's teacher says she is very bright and can attend any college she chooses.

EMBER MAI TRIMBLE, now thirty-something, got a pony for her seventh birthday and promptly started drawing horses. Later, when she was 12, she won a first place ribbon for riding her horse in a parade. Today, she still has a horse and continues to draw them, too. Her daughters, Delaney and Madison, also have artwork in the book.

MADISON MAI TRIMBLE has a great sense of humor and is always making people laugh. She's  very artistic and loves to draw, but also enjoys dance and takes ballet lessons. Some of her favorite activities are playing dress up and playing with her dolls. Madison is five.

JESSICA VAN ARSDALE has just started  fourth grade and is nine years old. She enjoys art class, where she primarily works in oils. Jessie is a basketball player, studies dance, and likes golf. She has had lots of pets, including a fuzzy rabbit and a noisy parakeet, but now has two dogs, Chipper Jones and Willie.

BROOKS WALLACE is start- ing high school, so he's naturally interested in cars and girls! He's 14, and recently purchased his first guitar with money that he earned himself.

ANNA WELLS, 12, is an avid doodler who specializes in fairies, frogs, and fantasy. She enjoys basketball, journaling, burning custom CDs for friends, and surfing the Internet. Anna has always considered herself an artist!

ACKNOWLEDGMENTS

First, my heartfelt thanks to all the artists who loaned me their works for this book—Anna, Brooks, Jessica, Madison, Ember, Delaney, Thomas T., Erika, Jaime, Jeremy, Dylan, Micah, Olivia P., Katrina, Corinna, Olivia M., Hannah, Miles, Triston, Brianna, Daniel, Quillan, Thomas G., Devon, Kayla, Karlie, Lucy, Django, Dana, and Terry—your artistry, imagination, and joy inspired me. You've made this a very special project.

I was fortunate enough to work with some very talented designers, who loved children's art and really understood the concept of the book. They created some very imaginative projects that truly honored the spirit and enthusiasm of the original works. So, thanks Stacey, Dietra, Dana, Corinne, Marthe, Diana, Radian, Pamela, Dyan, Allison, Terry, Jeanne, and Suzanne. I really appreciate your vision.

The good folks at Lark Books—editor Deborah Morgenthal, assistant editor Rain Newcomb, assistant art director Hannes Charen, art assistant Shannon Yokeley, art intern Lorelei Buckley, and project coordinator Terry Taylor—were tremendously helpful in bringing this vision of a book to reality. I'm especially grateful for the boundless talent and unbridled enthusiasm of art director Dana Irwin; she really believed in this book and is a true advocate for children's art. It's a beautiful book, Dana; thank you very much.

Photographer Keith Wright and his partner Wendy Wright are as delightful as they are talented, and I truly enjoyed working them. And we had a ball with our models: Carmin Charen, Dana Detweiler, Michael Foster, Margaret Murphy, Jaime Snyder, and Jessica Van Arsdale. They were kind enough to sacrifice a school holiday to come to the studio—and didn't complain! Thanks to you all; it was a lot of fun.

If I hadn't been blessed with little boys who drew shoes and trains and dragons and dinosaurs, I couldn't have written this book. They've grown up to become fine young men, and their lives are my greatest happiness. So, finally, I thank my sons Dylan and Jeremy, and dedicate this book to them. I love you.

INDEX